CAPTAIN COURAGEOUS
The Chris Hesketh Story

CHRIS HESKETH AND GRAHAM MORRIS

VERTICAL EDITIONS

First published in the United Kingdom in 2006 by
Vertical Editions, 7 Bell Busk, Skipton,
North Yorkshire BD23 4DT

www.verticaleditions.com

ISBN
1-904091-19-9
978-1-904091-19-6

Cover design and typeset by HBA, York

Printed and bound by the Cromwell Press, Trowbridge

CONTENTS

ACKNOWLEDGMENTS

The authors wish to acknowledge the valuable contributions of Tony Collins, Robert Gate and Michael Latham whilst compiling the statistical section of this book. Assistance provided by Ray French, John Riding and Paul Snape is also very much appreciated. Lastly, and certainly not least, thank you to Paul Charlton for so readily and enthusiastically agreeing to provide the foreword.

FOREWORD BY PAUL CHARLTON

I am delighted to be given the opportunity to write a few words on my old buddy, Chris Hesketh.

I joined Salford from Workington Town in 1969, two years after Chris had arrived at the club from Wigan, and it was during that period, prior to my arrival, that Chris played at Wembley in the 1969 Challenge Cup Final against Castleford. It was a match that really kicked off his career and even though Salford lost, he played so well that day he made people look up and take notice of him.

As well as being in the same team on countless occasions for Salford and Great Britain, we also played opposite to each other many times when I was playing for Workington Town or representing Cumberland. Very often, we were the opposing captains, meeting in the centre of the field to shake hands before the start. But whether we were on opposite sides of the field or not, my respect for him has always been the same.

For me, Chris is a born leader. When he puts his mind to doing something, he does it. He is a dedicated guy with whatever he does in life, and he got what he thoroughly deserved in being picked as captain of his country and receiving the MBE.

Chris and myself roomed together for much of the 1974 tour, something we had also done in France in 1972 when Great Britain won the World Cup. We were both dedicated players and we used to talk a lot about the game itself during that time in each others company. We were already good buddies but the bond between us became a lot stronger as a result of that experience.

We had full-time jobs in those days so training was not always that easy to manage. At Salford we always did what the coach told us, but then Chris and I always did that little bit extra. We both felt that if you wanted to stay at the top you had to make that extra effort and push yourself that little bit further.

Chris's story is an inspiration to anybody. He had polio when he was seven and it takes guts and determination to put that behind you and achieve what he has done in rugby league. His achievements should encourage anyone to fight for what they want out of life.

I consider it a privilege to have shared so many happy times with Chris both on and off the field.

Paul Charlton
Gold Coast, Australia
August 2006

INTRODUCTION

It is my firm belief that Chris Hesketh is the most outstanding Salford player of the post-Second World War period – and I have seen most of them. During his career at The Willows, the Red Devils had some extremely talented men on their register; wonderful entertainers of the calibre of David Watkins, speed merchants like Keith Fielding, skilful ball-players like Ken Gill and non-stop forwards like Colin Dixon. Chris, however, possessed an all-round ability and commitment that earned admiration throughout rugby league, qualities that brought him the captaincy of the 1974 British Lions. He was not what you would call a spectacular player – although his unorthodox sidestepping style was both unique and effective – but throughout his 12 seasons with Salford he proved himself a consistent performer who never gave less than 100% effort despite appearing in many a match when he was not fully fit. A solid defender, he brought leadership, inspiration and stability to the magical Salford side that Brian Snape's chequebook helped create from the late 1960s onward. Typical of Chris was the way he followed up every penalty kick on the off chance that it would ricochet off the post or a defender might fumble the ball. It was a ploy that came off in dramatic fashion at Station Road in 1971, collecting a rebound from the upright to run in the winning try in a vital League clash with Swinton and gaining Salford a crucial two points, a reward for dedication and perseverance.

Chris actually arrived at The Willows at the conclusion of the 1966/67 campaign, after transferring from Wigan. He was not a big name at the time, although he had played for the Great Britain Under-24 side. Nonetheless, his arrival in Weaste represented a major step up for Salford who had – with few exceptions – been bereft of players with any real pedigree since the glory days of the 1930s. I can vividly recall his first outing in a Salford jersey, appearing in a sevens tournament at Halifax in June 1967. Although precarious to draw too many conclusions from this miniaturised version of the game, I well remember his spectacular burst down the centre of the Thrum Hall pitch to score one of Salford's two tries in the opening round defeat by Oldham. I instinctively knew then that he was going to make an impact at The Willows and, for once, I was right. Despite the loss, I travelled home from Yorkshire that Sunday afternoon with quiet satisfaction after what I had witnessed from the young Wiganer.

I have long felt that Chris's story should appear in print. In terms of the history of the Salford club his impact was massive. Fourth in the clubs all-time appearances list, he took over the club captaincy from Watkins in 1974, leading his team to its second Championship of the decade in 1975/76. A World Cup winner in 1972, he has had more Test outings for Great Britain than any other Salford player and is the only representative of the club to tour more than once since their halcyon days of the 1930s.

In truth I never anticipated being the architect to his memoirs seeing the light of day, the seeds of which were sewn when I asked Chris if he would provide a foreword for another book I was working on. What should have been 20 minutes over a coffee soon became three hours and several coffees as, during our animated conversations, Chris became re-awakened to many of the experiences of his playing days.

Forthright and honest in his approach to rugby and life in general, he speaks very modestly about his own achievements. When, for example, he received the MBE in 1976 for services to Rugby League, his employer wanted to append the accolade to his business card, but Chris was not comfortable with the idea. So entertaining were his reminiscences, however, that I suggested: 'You should write your biography.' It was not a surprise to my ears when he retorted: 'Nobody would read it!' Thankfully, he was persuaded that the inspiring story of his rugby career – rising up as one of the 13-a-side codes biggest stars after being diagnosed at seven years of age as being unlikely to walk properly again and being discarded by his hometown Wigan club when he was 22 – is one that should be told.

I opted for the title of *Captain Courageous* as I believe it provides a perfect summation of his battle to overcome the challenges he has faced in sport and in life itself. Any doubts I harboured about that bold pronouncement receded when I recently re-read the souvenir brochure produced in 1978 for his joint testimonial with David Watkins. Inside was a eulogy to Chris from *The Sun's* Paul Harrison and guess what the headline was? That's right! So *Captain Courageous – The Chris Hesketh Story* it is! I hope you have as much pleasure reading it as I did in chronicling the tale with the great man himself!

Graham Morris
August 2006

1

JUST A WIGAN LAD!

Chris Hesketh never harboured an ambition to become a Rugby League player, let alone the codes first Wigan-born captain of a British Lions touring team. Raised within hailing distance of that former 'Mecca' of the 13 man game – the fondly remembered and much lamented Central Park –– he was just one of hundreds of youngsters living within the borough who packed the 'Hen-Pen' during the 1950s, usually on a cold, wintry Saturday afternoon, thrilling to the exploits of their cherry and white clad heroes. The idea of one day playing at Wembley Stadium or on Sydney Cricket Ground or receiving an MBE from the Queen would not have been part of his agenda. As far as Chris was concerned he was just a Wigan lad facing the challenges of life and trying to find his way in the world.

He was born Christopher Edwin Hesketh on 28 November 1944 at the family home situated above – and behind – the local fishmongers shop at number 53 Wigan Lane. 'I've shown the house to many people when driving past' says Chris, 'I just point up to the window and say "That's where I was born, in that bedroom up there!" If you went down our back ginnel – the way to get to our house – and were a cricketer with a good arm, you could throw a cricket ball from there onto the Spion Kop at Central Park!'

Chris's parents first set eyes on each other when they worked together at Timpson's shoe shop in Wigan, marrying in 1938. His father was named Thomas Clifford Hesketh although everybody, including Chris's mother, called him Cliff. He had previously lived

in the Beech Hill district of Wigan. In fact, all the family were
'Wiganers' although Chris's mother Winifred – otherwise known as
Winnie – could trace her roots to Ireland, her predecessors, like so
many others, having crossed the Irish Sea during the famine that
afflicted that country so badly in the latter part of the nineteenth
century. When Chris was a youngster, she worked at a wool shop
in Wigan to supplement the family income. Most of the time,
though, she was a housewife – after all there was four kids to look
after! There was Chris's elder brother Gerard, then came his sister
Monica, Chris himself, and younger brother Francis, who
everyone outside the family called Frank, including his wife. Chris
recalls that, when the family lived in Wigan Lane, Gerard would
make deliveries on his bicycle, which had a pannier on the front
and rear, to earn extra cash for the family:

My dad was a wonderful warm, friendly and funny man. It
was the biggest tragedy of my life when he died. I'm not
being disrespectful to anybody else but I miss him now and
think about him every day. When I was growing up it was
another era. To be honest I would rather not have done
anything other than what my dad wanted me to do, and that's
the God's honest truth. I didn't noticeably idolise him but he
was my dad and I respected him. I remember once, when I
was around 9 or 10, a mate of mine, Eddie Foster, and myself
were playing at the nearby graveyard and, of course, we
shouldn't have been. We were taking the white shiny pebbles
that you see on graves to use them for catapults. A policeman
came up and shouted 'Hey you!' Off we went and kept
running round this cemetery. He caught us eventually – he
caught me anyway – and he took me home. He knew my dad,
who was a special constable as well as his regular job. He
knocked on our door and I was stood there terrified. My dad
said 'What's going on here?' and the policeman replied 'Cliff,
he's done this' and 'he's done that.' My dad said 'Get up them

stairs now, you're not coming down' and that was it. My dad never hit me, or any of us really, although my mam sometimes did! When I was a little lad dad used to have a push-bike and I used to either go on the cross-bar or in a seat behind. You might think it funny for a bloke of my age but I still idolise my dad.

Chris was only seven years old when his whole future was placed in doubt, whilst his parents endured the most anxious and stressful period of their lives. It came in the midst of what had begun as a celebratory year for the Hesketh clan. Struggling to manage in the cramped conditions of their Wigan Lane home, their head count having reached six, they had their name down on the housing list for a council house. Finally, they got the exciting news that they had been allocated one at the new Norley Hall Estate in the Pemberton district.

Eventually, one day they all journeyed on the bus to take a look at it. What they saw were lots of houses rising out of the ground surrounded by old farm fields, close to the cemetery at St John's Church. At the time they did not know exactly which was going to be their house but Chris recalled thinking 'Wow! Indoor toilets! Bathrooms!' They were finally allocated number 77 Lamberhead Road. All the roads were named after places in the Lake District, Helvellyn Road, for example, was just around the corner. The floor of the hall and lounge had been covered with polished asphalt and there were three bedrooms and a bathroom, plus a sizeable back garden. 'To us it was a palace' says Chris, although, when they first moved in, the roads were unfinished being, effectively, just dirt tracks, whilst the pavements had kerbs set down but no flagstones:

We hadn't been in long – a couple of months or so – when I became ill. Where I contracted poliomyelitis, we think, was when my mam and dad and my other brothers and sister went to Blackpool for the day – like families did then – and we went on the beach. The sea had gone out but on the sands, next to the sea wall, there were puddles left by the sea and we paddled in them. They reckon that I could have caught it through having a cut on my leg or something, but nobody knew exactly.

The illness was like influenza and I was just being sick all the time. I was in bed and my mam kept coming in with all sorts of things. I was moved to the back bedroom for some reason, possibly to quarantine me, I don't know exactly why. The doctor came and I remember my mam saying to him 'Do you think its polio doctor?' because it wasn't uncommon at the time. I hadn't got a clue what polio was then. I wasn't bothered. I just wanted to get better. The doctor said 'I think it would be wise to take him into hospital' and even then I didn't think it was anything really serious. An ambulance came to take me to Whelley Hospital and I thought 'Blimey, this is going to be great – I'll be going out on a stretcher!' In actual fact, one of the ambulance men carried me over his shoulder in a blanket! The ambulance was outside with its light flashing and all the neighbours were watching, saying 'It's Christopher, I wonder what's wrong.' I got inside the ambulance and an ambulance man said to me 'I'll tell you what. When we're going through Wigan we'll put the bell on.' So, we're going through Wigan making siren noises and I was looking out through the ambulance window. I didn't really know how ill I actually was.

Chris was to spend the next ten months away from home and over a year out of school. Firstly, he was put into isolation in a glass unit at Whelley Hospital with doctors and nurses who attended him having to wear protective face-masks. Chris could walk, but with difficulty, the disease not only affecting his legs but his whole body. 'A girl in the next unit also had it but, unfortunately, she finished up in a wheelchair' recalls Chris. 'There was every chance

I could have had the same fate if it hadn't been for a vaccine that a certain Doctor Jonas Salk invented. I don't know whether it was that what saved me, or if it was God in Heaven and my mam praying a lot.'

When he left hospital, his next port of call was a convalescent home in Grange-over-Sands on the south Cumbrian coast, his recovery period being completed at another home on the Lytham St Annes coast road, run by nuns:

When I got back home, the Norley Hall Estate was all finished; tarmacked and flagged and everything – it looked great. I suppose I was still a bit delicate at the time due to the illness and I used to have to go to a clinic regularly with my mam and had to drink Minidex, which contained iron. I was out of school for a long while and was eight when I went back to St Cuthbert's in Mrs Riley's class – I was a big friend of her son Bernard who was a year or so older than me – and everybody in it could write except me!

Chris had only just moved to St Cuthbert's, in Pemberton, before his long absence, having transferred from St Mary's when his family relocated from Wigan Lane. St Mary's overlooked Wigan's Central Park ground. It had been his first school and was attached to St Mary's Church where Chris and his siblings were all baptised. It was at St Cuthbert's where Chris was to take up his favourite sport of rugby league, amazingly appearing in an inter-schools cup final only a few years after being confined to bed. His enthusiasm for the sport had begun when he was quite young, and still at Wigan Lane, Gerard having taken his younger brother to Central Park on many occasions to see the great stars of the day like Ken Gee, Brian Nordgren and Cec Mountford, who performed in front of massive crowds. The pair would watch their heroes from the junior enclosure known as the 'Hen-Pen', situated at the pavilion end next to where the players emerged from the tunnel onto the field. After moving to St Cuthbert's a young teacher called Joe McCardle, who lived in Whelley, emerged as Chris's first rugby mentor:

He had a moustache and to me he was a big grown up man, but he was only young. I think it was his first posting. We used to play 'tick and pass' at break time using a tennis ball, or we would go sidestepping up and down the school yard. To cut a long story short I think Joe McCardle must have seen something in me. I was sharp, I was quick and I was dodging everyone. I wasn't over big, but you didn't need to be in a school team did you really? The prop forwards were only the same size as me! He was in charge of all the rugby side of things and we had different age groups at the school. Eventually I started playing for St Cuthbert's – we wore green and white hoops like Glasgow Celtic – and we reached the Platt Cup Final at Central Park. I was 10 or 11 and we just lost – either 6-3 or 6-0 – to my old school, St Mary's. I remember that night at home I was distraught. I'd played at Central Park, which was what I always wanted to do, but we lost and I was crying my eyes out.

It was McCardle who was instrumental in Chris witnessing his first big match away from Central Park when they journeyed to Bradford's Odsal Stadium in April 1956 for a Wigan–Halifax Rugby League Challenge Cup semi-final clash:

He said to me 'Chris are you going to watch Wigan in the semi-final?' I replied 'No, I can't' and he said 'You can come with me on the train if you like.' I said 'All right' but it was not a question of me going home and somebody saying 'There's a pound to go.' What we kids used to do in those days was to go on the tip – there were plenty of tips around Wigan then! We would collect all the bottles and wash them and take them back to the shops to earn the three pence due back on them. Another time, myself and a mate of mine went up and down the posh part of Orrell, which is near Pemberton, and offered to do 'Bob-a-Job' but we weren't Boy Scouts at all! We got money for washing cars, mowing lawns, or whatever. Anyway, one way or another I got the money for the match and the train fare. I remember the train was packed and Odsal was crammed solid, it was incredible. I was so excited.

Unfortunately for Chris, and all the other Wigan fans that made the trip, his side failed to bridge its five-year Wembley gap, losing 11-10 in a match that resulted in Wigan's legendary winger Billy Boston almost ending his association with the club. Wigan officials suspended him for what they perceived as his lack of commitment for the tie, despite his scoring a try. Chris was almost nine years old the first time he saw Boston in action, as part of the phenomenal 8,500 crowd that turned up at Central Park on 31 October 1953, to see the Welshman's much heralded debut in an 'A' team fixture with Barrow. Thankfully, Boston's impasse with the club was resolved and he rescinded his threat to go back home to Cardiff and never to play for the 'Cherry and Whites' again. For Chris – a great admirer of Boston – it was a happy outcome, little realising he would partner his hero on Wigan's right flank eight years later.

At the time, Chris had never seriously cherished the thought of one day playing alongside his heroes on the hallowed Central Park turf. Although his brothers shared an interest in the game – and which schoolboy in Wigan didn't at the time? – there was no family pedigree that decreed his destiny was to reach the top in the toughest of all team sports:

To be honest, I never expected to play for Wigan. I was watching players from South Africa, New Zealand and Australia. To me it was incredible. I would go outside the

16

ground after every match with my autograph book and would get the same autographs every week! I'd be chasing them up and down the car park. They were the highlight of your life in those days. One minute you'd see Ken Gee coming out of the dressing room and then someone would say 'Hey, Joe Egan's over there.' You'd say 'I got him last week' but you'd still get him again though! I didn't have an idol as such, but then I moved on to watching David Bolton, a fabulous stand-off who was a Great Britain tourist in 1958 and 1962, and the great man who came from Tiger Bay – Boston. Both my brothers played rugby at school and afterwards Francis was involved for many years with the St Judes amateur club. To my knowledge, my dad, up until me playing in a school team, didn't ever bother. He wasn't a Wigan supporter as far as I can recall. He was a very good brass bandsman though, as is Gerard. They both played in several good brass bands. They tried to get me into it and I started playing the cornet at one time. I was 12 or 13. With everything else in my life then, I just couldn't do it, though I have often wished since that I had persevered.

The next phase in Chris's life began when he was eleven years old. Passing his school scholarship – the 11-plus as it was then called – brought with it a slight dilemma. Coming from a Catholic family he would normally have attended St Thomas More Secondary Modern School in Wigan had he failed his exams, but the options, having passed them, were more problematic! Chris recalled 'When I was taking the exam I didn't really know what it was. You've got to remember I was only a kid. How I did it I don't know, but I passed!' An alternative might have been to attend Wigan Grammar School, which was Protestant. 'It was no option at all as far as our family was concerned' says Chris. In fact there was no Catholic grammar school in Wigan at all. The nearest was West Park Grammar School in St Helens, and Thornleigh School at

Bolton. As the main road from Wigan to Ormskirk and St Helens went straight past the estate where he lived, West Park was chosen. He would take the number 362 bus, which conveyed him to St Helens town centre, transferring to a number 89 to complete his journey to the school.

Being educated at West Park brought about another change. If he was to continue playing rugby, he was going to have to switch codes, as his new school only offered rugby union, a sport he had not participated in previously. In charge of rugby activities at the school was Joe Coan, who later became coach at St Helens Rugby League Club, taking them to Wembley in 1966, Chris being a member of the Wigan squad that provided the opposition. Coan also found his way to Central Park, being responsible for team matters during the mid-1970s:

It was a big rugby school. I still played stand-off or centre as I always had and it wasn't a real change. I didn't really have a kicking game, but League-bred players generally didn't. I remember when David Watkins came to Salford from rugby union. In his first match he 'wellied' the ball about 70 yards and found touch in the corner and we said 'Keep your so-and-so feet off that ball! We want that ball in our hands, you've given it to them now.' 'I've just put you five yards off their line' he replied. 'Ay, but you've give them the so-and-so ball back' we said! At West Park when I got the ball from the scrum, I couldn't break my League habit and usually tried to take on and beat the opposing stand-off.

We had a lot of teams at West Park; under-12s, under-13s, under-14s, and so on. We had big playing fields and dressing rooms, a different world to me altogether. I remember when I went to the school the first time I had to get my school blazer and I'd never seen a blazer in my life before. That was a big item cost-wise for my mam and dad. I became known as the lad on our estate who had a satchel, a cap, and a lovely green blazer with a big badge on it with the motto 'Nisi Dominus Frustra', which means 'Without God All Is In Vain.' The school rugby kit was green and gold and in my five years there I don't remember us losing a match because we had such a good team. Peter Harvey and Keith Northey, who were a few years older than me – so I never played alongside them – were both head boys at West Park in their time, and both eventually went on to play for St Helens.

When Chris reached the age of 16 and was in his final weeks at school – he left in the summer of 1961 – it appeared as though he might have been saying farewell to his rugby activities, until fate took a hand. 'I was coming to the end of my time at school' says Chris, 'and there was a lad who I had played against at stand-off – I can't recall his name – and he got me to play for the West Park Old Boys. I quickly found myself playing in the first team with the grown-ups. I remember we went on a three-match tour to Cumberland. I was just a kid but the blokes were great with me. We won matches and I enjoyed it.'

Apart from continuing to play rugby after leaving school, there was another, more important task that needed his attention – that of obtaining employment and earning some money! He got himself fixed up with a job in the cost control department of a company called Triangle Valve, based in Pemberton. Chris recalled 'They had a rugby league team and Johnny Speed, a three-quarter who joined Swinton in the early 1960s, was with them. They played on Pemberton Rovers ground, which was an old ramshackle rugby league ground.' His first wage was £3 15s 2d (£3.76p) which, he remembers, was handed to him each week in a see-through packet. However, he was destined not to work there very long. Huddersfield Rugby League Club approached him through their forward Ted Slevin, a former Wigan player and member of their victorious 1951 Wembley side, prior to joining the Yorkshiremen. Chris had been spotted playing for West Park Old

Boys and invited to Huddersfield for a training session and to talk to club officials:

> I said to my dad 'I've got to go to Huddersfield for a trial but they won't let me off work.' So my dad said 'Take the day off' which was very irresponsible of him and me! I didn't know Ted Slevin at the time, except I knew he was a player who lived in the Wigan area, and he took me on the train. Huddersfield had a winger, a South African named Johannes De Klerk, who was out on the pitch training at the same time as me. I thought 'This is serious stuff this is! He's a real live South African and he's travelled all this way to play for them!'

Chris returned home from Huddersfield's former Fartown ground that evening, having experienced his first encounter with professional rugby league. He anticipated another call from the club, but heard no more about it. His midweek trip across the Pennines did have repercussions closer to home, however. 'I went into work the next day and they just said just "Go!" I've never been out of work since – thank God! I've had very little time off – only when I've had operations and stuff like that.' He fixed himself up with another job, working as a clerk for the William Park Company, an iron founders who operated at Wigan's Clarington Forge. He was still employed there at the time of his signing for Wigan in the spring of 1963 but, taking inspiration from his father, decided his future lay in sales.

His earliest memory of his father was that of being a gas fitter for the North West Gas Board, where he had also learned to drive. He eventually passed his driving test and drove round in a red Gas Board van. It had a 'crash gearbox' and occasionally his father would come home in it at a time when few people possessed a vehicle of any description:

> Anyone that owned a garage was considered 'dead posh.' A

lot of homes were having gas fires fitted at that time and he eventually became a salesman for the Gas Board. Being an outgoing person, he did well and, after several years, took another job as a representative for a builders' merchant. I thought to myself 'I wouldn't mind doing that.' I kept looking in the *Lancashire Evening Post* and the *Wigan Observer*, and the *Manchester Evening News* always had 'reps' jobs in it on Thursday night. I'd seen my dad do well as a salesman and he'd got a Cortina! I got a job with a firm called the Wigan Typewriter Company based in the Scholes area of Wigan. It was a little tiny shop. There was just the proprietor – I think his name was Eric – and a secretary upstairs. It was a little one front shop in a terrace and inside there were six or eight typewriters. He said 'Do you know anything about typewriters?' I replied 'Not really, but it's not exactly rocket science this is it?' For a couple of days I learned to type just two lines – 'Now is the time for all good men to come to the aid of the party' and 'The quick brown fox jumped right over the lazy dogs back' so I could go into an office or a shop, or whatever, and demonstrate.

I had no sales training at all. I'd knock on a door and show my business card and they'd either shut the window on me or I'd go inside. I got into doing it and thought 'I like this' but I couldn't drive. My dad started showing me how to drive in his company car, taking me to car parks or Southport beach so I couldn't hit anything! I also took some driving lessons with a little firm in Wigan at 17s 6d (87p) an hour. They shoved me in for my driving test and I passed it first time! I think it's because I was only 18 and had no fear! I went back to work and Eric said 'You're late!' I replied 'I've just been taking my driving test' and he said 'How did you go on?' 'I passed!' 'Right' he said, 'here's the keys to my blue Ford Anglia van!' Before then I had to go all over with a typewriter on the bus to places like St Helens and even into Liverpool.

With his own transport, Chris was able to get round to more customers – existing and potential – and his sales figures were gradually rising. One day a supplier came to the office to show Eric the latest development – electric typewriters! The visit stuck in Chris's mind for two reasons; it was the first time he had ever seen one and its demonstrator was to prove influential in his next career move:

I think he could see in me that I liked earning that commission! He took me on one side and said 'Are you all right working here?' and I said 'Yes'. He then said 'What do they pay you?' and I replied '£10 a week and commission.' He said 'There's a bigger company in St Helens called British and American Typewriters and they are looking for a rep and they'll pay you £12!' To cut a long story short, that's where I finished up in a little Austin A55 van to do my running about around St Helens and Merseyside. But I couldn't take the van home. I still had to get the train from Wigan to St Helens and back so I was paying out of this extra two quid to go on the train!

Returning to Chris's rugby exploits, he decided, having spent the 1961/62 season with West Park Old Boys, that it was time to find a club closer to home as he was still living in Pemberton on the Norley Hall Estate. 'Whilst I was at West Park Grammar School I always had a card – a bus pass in effect – so I didn't pay my fare' says Chris, 'When I left school and started playing for West Park Old Boys – whose ground was on Prescott Road and not far from St Helens Rugby League Club – I couldn't really afford, financially, to keep playing and training with them. I was 17 and, it might sound petty now, but then I don't remember having any money at all.' Reluctantly Chris said farewell to West Park and joined the Orrell Rugby Union Club, playing for the Colts team.

Chris was to spend just one season – 1962/63 – at Orrell. Still in his teens, he was beginning to make people – particularly rugby league scouts – sit up and take notice of his capabilities as an inside back. He had developed a rather unorthodox style when it came to outwitting defenders, and – to the untrained eye – he sometimes gave the impression that, having beaten three opponents, he would step back into the 'traffic' and try and beat them again!

Eric Ashton, when he was my coach at Wigan, used to say 'Chris you've just beaten that man superbly and then you come back and you're trying to beat him again.' And I knew – I always did know – that I over-sidestepped and did things like that. To be honest a lot of it was down to the fact that at West Park Grammar School, St Cuthbert's before that, and at home in the streets – and I'm not joking – we played 'tick and pass' a lot and you literally had to evade people and I just developed my style through that. I remember my brother Gerard and I used to go round to Robin Park – not far from where we lived – and about ten of us played regularly. I was trying to be elusive, basically to get out of the way and that's where I got this rocking from side-to-side running motion. I was not aware of having a different style. I just thought I was a centre or stand-off who could go and beat my opponent. But I didn't copy anybody. When I was at stand-off you could never measure me against David Bolton for example, because he would get the ball, run straight, and try and get outside his opposite stand-off. I always used to think, when there was a scrum, if that ball comes to me 'What am I going to do?' and that stuck with me through my career. It didn't always work mind!

When I was playing in the centre at Salford I'd be thinking 'Who was I operating against?' Say, for example, it was Leeds' centre Syd Hynes. If he was playing against me he'd stand two yards wide of me. He'd say 'You're not coming round me because it's too far and if you come inside you're getting hit hard' and so you said to yourself 'What should I do here?' Probably if Hynes is standing wide, I'd say to our full-back Paul Charlton 'Charlo, I'll run at the inside centre and you come straight off my shoulder because there's going to be a bit of a gap between there and Hynes.' Charlo may well have got a thump – and with Hynes there was every likelihood – but that's the way we talked about it and played it.

It was during Chris's solitary season at Orrell that he received further approaches from professional outfits. This time the interested parties were St Helens and Warrington. Chris cannot remember exactly how he got invited to St Helens but recollects the strange feeling of being on their training pitch – situated in front of the main entrances to their Knowsley Road ground – watched by around 50 spectators and 'Training with well-known players I would normally be on the terraces watching.' Warrington – coached at the time by Ernie Ashcroft, a star centre for Wigan in the years following the Second World War – had Tommy Conroy and Jackie Melling, two Wigan lads, on their playing staff. 'It might have been through Tommy – who lived just around the corner from me in Pemberton – that I got invited to Warrington, I'm not exactly sure' says Chris. Just over six years later, Chris, then playing for Salford, would oppose the pair in one of the biggest matches of his life, the 1969 Challenge Cup semi-final at Central Park.

He only trained a couple of times with St Helens and Warrington and, as with his Huddersfield trip, there was no instant follow-up. 'People would have said to me "Are you coming training at Warrington next week?" or wherever. I was only a young lad and, naively perhaps, I wasn't even thinking they might sign me.' Whatever his own thoughts at the time about the apparent rejection of his talents, it was only a temporary blip in his rugby career. Although, not aware of it, other eyes had been observing him and a dream move lay just around the corner.

2

WIGAN CALLING!

For most teenagers at the time, 1963 represented the year that the sound of 'Merseybeat' groups dominated the hit parade, Gerry and the Pacemakers being the first of the new-wave Liverpool acts to hit the summit with *How Do You Do It?* during April. For 18-year-old Chris Hesketh, however, that particular month was a big hit in a completely different way, the youngster making his debut in Wigan's famous cherry and white jersey.

His sporting life was to change forever on Saturday 27 April 1963 after appearing in an end-of-season rugby union seven-a-side tournament for Orrell at the Newton-le-Willows Grammar School ground. Most of the Orrell seven that day were first team players, including the likes of Des Seabrook, a well known name in rugby union at that time who appeared 38 times for Lancashire. It was the performance of Chris, however, that was observed by one rugby league spy. As he left the field for the final time, heading in the direction of the changing rooms, a small man wearing a trilby sauntered up to him. It was Billy Mercer, a St Helens scout who played for the Saints at Wembley in 1930 as centre to legendary wingman Alf Ellaby:

> He said 'How do you fancy playing for St Helens?' I was still in my kit and looking forward to getting changed. 'Will you come for a trial next Wednesday? If you do, be at Knowsley Road at half past six.' I got home and I mentioned it to my mam and dad and they said 'Blimey! Playing for St Helens!' But when I came home the next night, Jack Wood, the Wigan

secretary, had rung and asked 'Will Chris Hesketh go for a trial for Wigan on Monday night?' So that's what I did. I went to Wigan instead. There was no choice as far as I was concerned!

So it was that on Monday 29 April Chris turned out as a trialist in the Wigan 'A' team against Warrington 'A' at Central Park, a match that the home side comfortably won 36-5. He clearly made an impression. The following day's edition of the *Wigan Observer*, under the headline 'Signed After One Trial' said 'After watching him play a trial in their A team against Warrington last night, Wigan Rugby League club signed on professional forms 18-year-old Orrell RU Club Colts stand-off Chris Hesketh. Wigan have had an eye on Hesketh for over 12 months and after making first overtures nearly a year ago they decided to let him mature. Now they have had their hand forced by keen interest shown by several other clubs. Seven club directors watched him in action last night.'

After the match they dragged me into a room with my dad. We spoke to club director Billy Wood. Bert Webster, the chairman, was also there, but Wood did the talking. He said 'We'll give you £200 less tax' which came to £146, and my dad had to sign the agreement because I wasn't old enough. If they had been watching me for a year, I didn't know about it.

The Beatles had displaced Gerry with their first number one *From Me To You* by the time Chris made his second appearance on Wednesday 15 May, another 'A' team fixture at Central Park. The home side, reportedly, produced 'fast, open rugby that overwhelmed Oldham' the score being 47-5. It was noted in the local press that 'Wigan half-backs Chris Hesketh and Johnny Phillips had outstanding games, with Hesketh scoring three tries.' Scrum-half Phillips, signed from St Helens amateur rugby league a few years earlier, was, despite the promising oratory, destined to make a lesser impact at Wigan than Chris, earning just four first team appearances. The 15 May was also the date that Chris signed his official contract with Wigan, its preparation hindered no doubt by club officials' pre-occupation with the senior squad's visit to Wembley the previous weekend. It was their fourth Challenge Cup Final in six seasons, Wakefield Trinity getting the better of them on this occasion.

When Chris arrived at Central Park, Griff Jenkins was in charge of the team. Although born in Warrington, Jenkins claimed Welsh ancestry, his father, a former rugby union player from the valleys, having played scrum-half for the Wilderspool club before the First World War. Jenkins was, subsequently, raised in Wales, playing rugby union for Pen-y-graig and Weston-super-Mare, before signing professional with Warrington in 1934 and representing his home-town team on the wing in the 1936 Challenge Cup Final at Wembley. He had taken the helm at Wigan in 1961 – having built his reputation as coach of the great Oldham team of the 1950s – but, when Chris arrived, Jenkins' days at the club were numbered:

I was in heaven. I was only young and playing and training with blokes like Billy Boston, Eric Ashton and Trevor Lake. At the time, I used go to my grandma's after work and she'd always give me an apple. I was going training on Tuesday and Thursday and, walking into the dressing room one evening, I remember Boston saying to me 'You're not eating that apple and then going out training?' I said 'I'm hungry!' He was telling me I shouldn't eat anything before training. I don't know if that had anything to do with it, but on one occasion, Jenkins took me back to the dressing room from one training session. I was, apparently, looking so pale he was worried I was going to keel over, although I felt great. They had me checked out by the physiotherapist, Jack Alstead, and that would be due to Griff. I'd be sprinting, doing moves and press-ups and I think it was perhaps because I was so slender at the time and trying hard. I suppose Griff noticed I was looking a bit drained. I was thinking 'I hope they're not going to stop me playing' because I felt fine.

Having played two 'A' team games, Chris's season was effectively over and, following the close season break, he reappeared several months later with the rest of the Wigan squad for pre-season training in the build up to the 1963/64 campaign. As was customary with most clubs at that time, Wigan staged a pre-season public trial match on Saturday 10 August 1963. It was a landmark afternoon for Chris, who began the match playing for the 'Blues', composed of 'A' team backs and first team forwards, against the 'Cherry and Whites', who contained first team backs and 'A' team forwards. Chris was picked at left centre, his winger being Jim McCormack, who later joined Oldham, where he made over 150 appearances.

The Blues led 30-0 at half-time, Chris giving such a good account of himself that he was switched to the 'Cherry and Whites' for the second period, linking up with the senior backs as stand-off partner to former Oldham star and ex-Great Britain international, Frank Pitchford. With Chris in their side the Cherry and Whites reduced the final deficit to 41-30, the *Wigan Observer* headline announcing 'New Boys Shine In Trial', a reference to Chris and 16-year-old back Kevin O'Loughlin, who was also to have a rewarding rugby league career. The *Wigan Observer's* knowledgeable and respected writer Jack Winstanley said 'Two of Wigan's newest players provided many of the highlights of the club's public practice match' going on to state that at centre or stand-off, Hesketh 'showed some nice touches from both positions.'

The *Wigan Observer* again promoted his name with the headline 'Hesketh Wins Place', readers being informed that 'On the strength of an impressive performance in the public practice match, former Orrell RU Club colt Chris Hesketh wins the stand-off berth in the Wigan team to play Warrington in the annual Wardonia Charity Cup match at Central Park this Saturday.' Although classed as a friendly fixture rather than a 'competitive' match, the pre-season clash, which began in the 1930s, was effectively Chris's first team debut. Staged at Central Park on 17 August, Chris, although on the wrong end of a 31-5 score-line, again caught the eye of Winstanley, who wrote 'Considering that he was making his first senior appearance for Wigan, young stand-off Chris Hesketh didn't make a bad job of it. He made a nervous looking start in dropping several passes, but his game thereafter was an industrious one and not without its good moments.'

With barely a month of the season gone, Wigan captain Ashton took over as player–coach, Jenkins being removed from office following some disappointing results during September. Chris would, however, renew his acquaintance with Jenkins a few years later:

Eric Ashton was a good coach. He wasn't a shouter, except for shouting certain moves or something like that. He was more of a thinker. Eric was a really good person to be with. Although he was captain of Great Britain he had no ego. I used to look up to him. I'd think to myself 'He's been to Australia and New Zealand and done it.' I remember travelling long distances on the team coach to places like Workington, Whitehaven, Barrow and Hull and some would be playing cards, some would be chatting. I remember – two or three times – players reminiscing about the 1962 tour and I'd say 'What's it like in Australia?' Listening to them talking about their experiences made me more and more determined to eventually be selected to tour Australia and New Zealand myself.

Chris spent the early months of his first campaign playing in the 'A' team, mostly at centre, patiently waiting until 30 November for his official senior debut, a Western Division Championship match at Leigh. With regular stand-off Bolton indisposed, he was brought in to replace Stan McLeod – following a 'disappointing' 8-8 home draw with Workington Town the previous week – as partner to Frankie Parr. The Wigan team read: Boston, Carlton, Ashton, Davies, Lake, Hesketh, Parr, Barton, Sayer, McTigue, Lyon, J Stephens, Gilfedder. Commenting on Chris's performance in his match report, Winstanley said 'He was at his best when running individually from broken field play, and he showed courage in both attack and defence.' Despite his endeavours, Leigh triumphed 20-7. During his four years at Wigan, Chris made 23 of his 74 starts in official fixtures at outside-half, 17 with Parr alongside him. 'Frankie Parr was from Leigh' says Chris, 'He lived very close to the Sportsman's pub that Griff Jenkins used to run. I was quite friendly with Frank and we'd often go for a pint after training, although I remember he always wanted to go on the slot machines! He was a good scrum-half and I'm surprised he never won international honours.'

It was not until the following February that Chris got his next opportunity. He must have thought he was dreaming as he took his place in a three-quarter line that read Boston-Ashton-Hesketh-Lake. It was far from a vintage Wigan performance, the Cherry and Whites taking the spoils 12-7 against a determined Liverpool City at Knotty Ash. Winstanley pulled no punches in condemning the sides overall performance, particularly the two teenagers in their midst, although conceding it was 'sad for new boys Chris Hesketh at left centre and 16-year-old Kevin O'Loughlin at stand-off. Both are young enough to learn and inexperience itself can often lead to mistakes – but they undoubtedly warrant quite severe criticism for the way they repeatedly turned inside and hung on to the ball when it would have been better and more advantageous to pass. Their displays clearly reflected the difference they found in the speed of A team football opposed to senior grade rugby.'

His words were vindicated with both being absent the following week. Chris, though, would get further chances to renew his partnership with Rhodesian flyer Lake, the pair eventually appearing together a dozen times on Wigan's left flank, although the second occasion was almost a year away. 'Trevor Lake came to Wigan with another Rhodesian, John Winton, a full-back who finished up at Oldham' says Chris, 'Lakey was a great winger. He was like lightning, a real class player and of course he had that wonderful final at Wembley in 1965 when he scored those two marvellous tries against Hunslet.'

Meanwhile, Chris was making quite a name for himself in the Wigan 'A' team who, along with the Warrington reserves, were battling it out at the top of the Lancashire Combination. In one match, against Salford 'A' at Central Park on Saturday 18 January, he scored four tries and created another two for his wing Frank Carlton 'after outstanding centre play' as they walloped their unfortunate visitors 56-3. Wigan 'A' did not ultimately take the title, but they did reach the Lancashire Shield Final, Chris scoring two of the tries that helped overcome a determined Whitehaven challenge by 16-0 in the semi-final at Central Park on 1 February. The draw favoured rivals Warrington for the Final, the deciding match between the two pace-setters taking place at Wilderspool on Saturday 14 March. The result was a disappointing 15-5 defeat, although Chris – who had 'stood out' – had the satisfaction of claiming his first medal in professional rugby league. The Wigan team was: McLeod, Lindley, McCormack, Hesketh, Magnall, O'Loughlin, Pitchford, Belshaw, Clarke, Larkin, Woosey, A Stephens, Sharrock.

Chris got the chance to redeem himself in the senior team when returning at the end of March for a home meeting with Hunslet. It commenced a run of six first team games as the season wound down, the first five being at stand-off in place of Bolton, who relocated to the centre. The match, a 31-4 victory over the south Leeds side, was also a personal triumph for Chris, putting his downbeat show of the previous month well and truly behind him, with a five-star three-try performance. The *Wigan Observer* headline proclaimed a 'Hesketh Hat Trick' – his only one for the Wigan first team – its journalist boldly stating 'Hesketh looked better at stand-off than Bolton had done recently' Chris's first try-scoring effort followed a spectacular penetrating run by left wing pairing Lake and Alan Davies, the latter transferring the ball inside for him to race over. Loose forward Roy Evans, who 'scattered a ragged Hunslet defence', set up his second, Chris initiating the third himself from the Wigan 25-yard line, subsequent quick handling from Brian McTigue, Bolton, Boston and Brian Shillinglaw, enabling him to complete his trio:

I've still got a framed picture of myself going under the posts against Hunslet. I look like a little lad on it and I'm not joking! It was played on an Easter Monday. I was supposed to be playing in the A team that day and my mam said there'd been a phone call for me and could I get to Central Park. I was in the A team most of the time in my first two seasons. I was a 'Jack of all trades', the bloke they dragged in at full-back, wing, centre or stand-off!

Former Scotland rugby union international, Shillinglaw, partnered Chris throughout his five-match sequence at half-back. The following weekend, in a 38-12 hammering of Hull at the Boulevard, the pair clearly gelled, one scribe saying 'Shillinglaw and Hesketh had a hey-day making good use of all possession from the scrum.' Lake ran in four tries whilst Chris scored his fourth of the season after evading three defenders on a 40-yard run to the try line. He could easily have made it a brace as he also crossed the whitewash earlier but failed to ground the ball properly. Chris's final match of that run – against fierce rivals St Helens at Central Park on 22 April – is probably the one he took most pride in, as it was the first of three occasions when he was centre to boyhood hero Boston. Although his partnership with Boston produced a try for the wingman, it was not enough to prevent a 22-13 loss:

Billy really helped me. If I dropped the ball he would say to me 'It's ok, catch it next time!' People say to me now 'Oh, are you from Wigan? That's who that Billy Boston used to play for, he's a big fellah.' But he wasn't a big fellah when he first came, he was built like a stick and was like lightning, nobody could put a finger on him. He ran all over the field and when he found a gap no one could catch him. I remember seeing Wigan beat Dewsbury 52-5 in the opening match of the 1955/56 season and he got seven tries and one headline said 'Dewsbury Spill Milk At Boston Tea Party.' For some reason that has always stuck in my mind.

Billy Boston was 'Mister Wigan' really and a wonderful shy man. I know Billy had his fall-outs with Wigan but he is the most charming of men. Talk about humility, its humility gone mad with Billy. If you were lucky you'd see Billy walking through the town to the match from Poolstock, where he lived, wearing his club blazer. I don't like saying things like 'The greatest ever' but I never saw a better winger than Billy Boston and I certainly never met a nicer fellah – he is a class man.

David Bolton played his last match for the club in April 1964, moving to Australia during the summer, where he joined Balmain. Any possibility of Chris stepping into the international stand-off's boots during the 1964/65 term were scuppered through the arrival of Cliff Hill. The talented back was signed from Newton-le-Willows Rugby Union Club in May 1964 and quickly made the outside-half berth his own. His impact was such that he represented both Great Britain and Lancashire in only his second season in the top flight:

I suppose Cliff Hill coming to Wigan was bad news for me.

Eric Ashton liked Cliff. He wasn't the same type of player as I was. He was a purist stand-off, a silky player. He took the ball and he got the back line moving and he backed up – he was classy. I was more rugged and a harder tackler. You didn't get Cliff tackling like that, but he'd always be on the end of a pass. I'm not knocking anything about him and I always got on very well with him. I knew he was a better player than me at stand-off for Wigan. I was too tight with the ball to be honest. I wanted to get hold of it and beat three men and run 60 yards and score. But that was naivety and youth – I just wanted that ball! Eric Ashton said to me 'You're the only player I know that can sidestep in mid-air.' Sometimes it would have been better if I'd just got the ball from the scrum-half, ladled it on and brought the full-back in outside the second centre, or whatever.

The 1964/65 campaign opened with Wigan staging their, then, annual pre-season sevens tournament on Bank Holiday Monday, 3 August, for the Silcock Cup. Chris was included in the home line-up, chipping in with two vital tries in a closely fought 11-8 win over St Helens at the semi-final stage, Wigan winning the competition through outscoring Halifax 15-11 in the final. He also appeared at stand-off for the opening 13-a-side fixture, the Wardonia Cup clash with Warrington, held this time at Wilderspool on 15 August, Wigan winning 9-8.

In what was the first season for allowing substitutes – although only until half-time and for injured players to begin with – Chris found himself on the bench for the opening League fixture at Swinton seven days later, but did not enter the fray. After that he disappeared from the squad for several months, languishing in the 'A' team, where he was picked mostly at centre with the occasional match at stand-off, whilst Hill became virtually an ever-present as the first team out-half.

His next first team chance came during a home match with

Widnes in mid-November, demonstrating his versatility by coming off the substitutes bench to replace the injured Ray Ashby at full-back. With Ashby still indisposed, he started as the last line of defence for the following weekends trip to Oldham, making a big impression. Winstanley, in the *Wigan Observer*, described his display in glowing terms, noting that he 'scored a remarkable solo try 11 minutes from the end. (Oldham winger Mike) Elliott dropped the ball 10 yards inside the Wigan half. Boston picked up and gave to Hesketh. A try from such a position must have been beyond anybody's wildest dream – but that was precisely what resulted from the full-back's corkscrew run covering more than 50 yards. He bounced into and out of three tackles before touching down near the corner flag.' The try came at just the right moment for the visitors, his three-pointer killing off a spirited Oldham revival, Wigan going on to win 18-9.

Chris's next opportunity to shine came a few weeks later with six consecutive matches through November and December, plus another outing in mid-February. All were in the three-quarter line – both wing and centre – where he covered, in turn, the absences of established stars Boston, Davies and Keith Holden. He was recalled again for the final two League fixtures, played during April, this time at stand-off, briefly renewing his collaboration with Parr, Hill being unavailable. Hill was to reclaim his place, however, for the last, and most important, match of Wigan's season – the spellbinding win over Hunslet at Wembley. Chris's name was absent from the 16-man panel that travelled down to London, although it was not a complete surprise and the omission did not bother him unduly.

It was the 1965/66 season that provided the breakthrough for Chris in that he was in Wigan's fifteen for all but one of their 47 matches. It was also a campaign that confirmed his tag at Central Park of being a utility player, appearing in every back position from one to six:

I would play anywhere really. And I did; I played on both wings, I played both centres, full-back and stand-off. Being called a utility player wasn't a problem in the slightest. From being a little lad watching Wigan, and living so near as well, the club was just a big part of my life. I never imagined that, first of all, I would play for Wigan, and then, when I did play for Wigan, I never imagined that I would play for anybody else. Of course that eventually happened, although it was to my benefit as it turned out. I never bothered where I played so long as I was playing.

On 4 September, he received plaudits for his performance at stand-off half against the New Zealand touring team, earning the 'Man of the Match' award – sponsored by Benson & Hedges cigarettes – in the process. 'I've still got the silver pen I received' says Chris, who took the accolade in atrocious, muddy conditions that made running and handling difficult. A caricature of Chris subsequently appeared in a cartoon strip of the match – drawn by 'Edge' – in the local *Post and Chronicle*. The caption read: 'Chris Hesketh richly deserved his £10 Benson and Hedges best player award. Considering what he went through they wouldn't have got us on for £10,000 and a ten ton load of fags thrown in free!'

Winstanley was clearly impressed with Chris's form against the tourists, who won 17-12, making the following bold prediction: 'Although I feel Hesketh will be hard pressed to win international recognition this season, his value as a utility player may well stand him in good stead when the Great Britain party to tour Australia is named next year. I have seen him fill the roles of full-back, wing, centre and stand-off with great credit over the past two years. His elusiveness and strength in both attack and defence earned him top marks in this display.' Although he did not fulfil that prophesy for the upcoming 1966 tour, Chris proved Winstanley a sound judge when making the cut four years later.

He did not have to wait quite that long, though, for

'international recognition', being selected as back substitute for the Great Britain Under-24s team to take on their French counterparts at Oldham's Watersheddings enclosure on 20 October 1965. The British line-up, which won 12-5, was: Tyrer (Leigh), Thomas (Featherstone Rovers), Major (Hull Kingston Rovers), Maloney (Hull), Wear (Barrow), Millward (Castleford), Prosser (St Helens), Tonks (Featherstone Rovers), K Taylor (Oldham), B Taylor (Dewsbury), Kirkbride (Workington Town), Gaines (Keighley), Robinson (Swinton). Substitutes: Hesketh (Wigan), Irving (Oldham). Chris was called upon to replace Major in the centre although it is not a match that he recalls with any clarity. He does, however, retain fond memories of the opposing loose-forward Jean-Pierre Clar. 'He became captain of France and I played against him several times when I was a full international. He always greeted me with "Esket! Bonjour!" whenever we met in France and I shared a few pints with him' says Chris.

The climax of the 1965/66 campaign saw Wigan visit Wembley for their sixth Challenge Cup Final appearance since 1958. Chris sat it out on the substitutes bench in the wins over Halifax in the first round and Bradford Northern in the third, but started the second round tie against Whitehaven at Central Park as centre to Boston. Chris and his illustrious partner scored a try apiece in the 40-6 win. He also appeared as substitute for Parr in the 7-2 semi-final success over Leeds at Huddersfield. It was his last taste of action in that year's competition, however, not being required to vacate his seat on the sidelines during the Final which arch-rivals St Helens won convincingly 21-2, Wigan being badly handicapped through the absence, due to suspension, of hooker Colin Clarke:

To be honest I was just thrilled to be on the bench for Wigan at Wembley. We stayed near Wembley in Hendon at the Hendon Hall Hotel. The evening before the final, Eric Ashton read the team out and said I was on the bench. That was it as far as I was concerned. I didn't go to my room and sulk or anything. After all, I was still only 21, and you can't believe how I enjoyed the experience of just going training with the likes of Billy Boston, Eric Ashton and Brian McTigue. As far as I was concerned Eric was the coach and I had such an admiration for him. But, obviously, he didn't rate me as much as he rated Cliff Hill, and one or two others whose positions I might have filled at that time.

Chris started in 31 matches during 1966/67, but a mid-season fall from grace cost him his place in what was, arguably, Wigan's biggest match of the season; the Lancashire Cup Final victory over Oldham at Swinton on 29 October. He had played in the opening two rounds but, as John Benn, writing in the *Wigan Observer*, announced in his preview to the Final: 'Hesketh, who had an outstanding full-back game at Oldham, has again been excluded from the panel of 15.' Chris was picked as the travelling reserve – effectively the 16th man – although he still received his winners' medal. Benn's reference to Chris's 'outstanding' performance was for the League fixture at Watersheddings on 30 September, when he had filled in admirably once more for an absent Ashby as the last line of defence. After featuring in the opening 14 matches of the campaign, though, he suddenly found himself sat idly on the sidelines with a number '14' on his jersey, or playing in the 'A' team:

> I perhaps got a bit peeved sometimes because at that time you could be on the bench and you couldn't always come on. I suppose they saw me as a wing or centre then. I would never complain. I would have played hooker for Wigan if they'd asked me to. I just wanted to play rugby. It wasn't about the money. It wasn't about the glory. It was true then, and all through my career, including my time at Salford. It wasn't like the glory that players have now. You were just working lads who did a job in the day and trained twice a

week, with possibly an extra one, and played the matches at weekend. That's why I loved my time at Salford so much because you'd walk off the pitch and the spectators were really your friends. A lot of them actually were – you just made friends with people.

It was during this period, on 26 November, that he was selected a second time for the Great Britain Under-24s, being required to travel across the channel to Bayonne, situated close to the Spanish border in south-west France. Britain lost 4-7 with Chris, again picked as the back substitute, joining the fray to play in three different positions during a match described as 'near farcical.' Harold Mather, in *The Guardian*, wrote: 'Many of (referee) Mr (Edouard) Martung's decisions defied comprehension', a reference to the French scoring the only try of the match from a blatant forward pass and the unfathomable dismissal of Wigan prop John Stephens. Mather did, however, note that 'Hesketh, who took the place of (Jack) Gamble (Castleford) just before half-time, made several good breaks.'

The following weekend, Wigan entertained Blackpool Borough at Central Park. Chris was not selected – not even as substitute – but was chosen instead to play at full-back for Wigan's 'A' team, due to meet Blackpool's reserves in the famous seaside resort. Two weeks later, on Friday 16 December, under the headline 'Hesketh Is Back – On The Wing' an intriguing story appeared in the *Wigan Observer*. It read: 'Chris Hesketh, the Great Britain Under-24s international utility back, who flatly refused to turn out in the A team a fortnight ago and escaped disciplinary action, is on Wigan's left wing against Widnes under the Naughton Park floodlights tonight. The versatile Hesketh made his stand when he was left out of the first team panel for the match against Blackpool Borough. Last weekend he was not picked for the first team (at Liverpool City) and was ineligible for the A team Lancashire Cup Final. But on Monday night, Wigan took the unexpected step of naming him to take over from the injured David Stephens.' Although the report looks to be quite well informed, its content is a complete mystery to Chris who says 'I don't remember ever, in all of my career, refusing to play for anybody in any position. I was just not that kind of player.'

Stephens – signed from Castleford Rugby Union Club – had taken over the left wing berth after Lake departed to join Australian club St George, his last Wigan match being the Lancashire Cup Final. Stephens' injury kept him out for the rest of the season and Chris – beginning with the match at Widnes – was to play in the remaining 18 games of the campaign. All but two – at stand-off – were on the left flank, usually with Ashton or Holden as his centre.

It was during this run of matches, that Chris received news that hit him like the proverbial bolt out of the blue and led, ultimately, to his exit from Central Park. Wigan had slid dramatically to the lower half of the 30-team Championship table, having ended the previous campaign in the top three. For the past four seasons the goal-kicking responsibility had sat squarely on the shoulders of former Warrington second-row or loose-forward Laurie Gilfedder but club officials had clearly decided a new marksman would assist the club's resurrection. Colin Tyrer, a prolific goal scorer for neighbours Leigh, seemed to fit the bill. The adventurous, attacking full-back had been a team-mate of Chris's in both his Under-24s international appearances, and, reportedly, had fallen out with Leigh coach Alex Murphy and, therefore, anxious for a change of club.

Chris knew little of what was happening behind the scenes until one day, during February 1967, he was enjoying a pint and 'putting the world to rights' with Blackpool Borough's Australian second-row forward Bill Cane, at a pub in Standish. Cane previously played for North Sydney and originally journeyed to England to join Wigan a few years earlier, but had only managed to prise their first team door open once, during 1965:

Two Wigan Rugby League directors walked in fully 'trilby-ed' up. The place was empty and I said to Bill 'Eh up, what are those two after?' They got their drinks and sat down in another part of the pub. I think one of them was Harry Gostelow and the other was the chairman, Bert Webster. They motioned me to go over and I went across and sat down. Instinctively, I said 'Now then, who do you want to swap me for?' and they looked at one another amazed. 'Well how did you know that?' one of them said. I replied 'Oh, come on – I'm a big lad!' They said something like 'Chris, we need a goal-kicking full-back' and straight away I said 'Tyrer!' I was not interested in what they were proposing and told them so, and thought that was it. But, the next time we went training, on the top field behind the Spion Kop as usual, Eric Ashton brought it up again, saying 'Chris, Leigh's been on for you.' I said to my dad 'I don't want to go to Leigh' – apparently Alex Murphy wanted me – and my dad said 'Well don't go!' I said 'It's all right saying that, but it will make my life even worse at Wigan.' I had more or less burnt my bridges. I said 'No' which meant Wigan had to buy Tyrer for about six grand. So Wigan got their goal kicking full-back but my days were numbered.

Sure enough, in their Friday, 3 March edition, the *Wigan Observer* reported: 'Colin Tyrer, Leigh's Under-24s international full-back, became a Wigan player on Wednesday night. Initially, Leigh were willing to talk business provided Wigan's versatile utility back Chris Hesketh was involved in the deal. But, as anticipated, Hesketh refused to move to Hilton Park. He reported to Central Park in mid-afternoon on Tuesday (28 Feb) to meet Leigh secretary Alderman Tom Hourigan and other directors. But they failed to persuade him to change his mind and, after negotiations lasting three and a half hours, Wigan agreed to a straight cash deal.' Chris, referred to in the newspaper as being 'somewhat upset' was quoted, at the time, as saying 'I don't want to leave Wigan. I was staggered when I heard it was proposed that I should. I was just finding my feet clinching a regular first team place.' With the dye being cast for Chris the moment he refused to be the makeweight in the Tyrer deal, it was no real surprise when he was transferred out of Central Park a few months later:

> It was nice to know that Murphy wanted me to go to Leigh, albeit in part exchange, and if I had gone, perhaps I would have been in the Leigh team that won the Challenge Cup against Leeds at Wembley in 1971, you never know. You look back on these things but it's a funny old game isn't it? In refusing to go to Leigh, though, my card was marked because Wigan had to pay for Tyrer. I felt very disappointed. Like any lad who wanted to play for Manchester United or Manchester City or whatever, I wanted to play rugby for Wigan. That's where I came from and that's my grounding. It also implies you're not good enough for the team, which revs you up when you go somewhere else and play against them. All it did with me – and this is the sort of person I am whether its rugby or work or whatever – it gave me more determination to succeed. I didn't get up every morning saying 'I'm going to show Wigan', I trusted my actions would speak louder than words, which hopefully they did do.

3

HEADED IN THE RIGHT DIRECTION

The 1966/67 season that, for two-thirds of the campaign, had given Chris optimism for a bright and sunny future at Central Park, was coming to a dismal, cloudy end. The gloom had gathered in his mind since being shaken by the Colin Tyrer 'incident' that began in February and, at 22 years old, his Wigan dream seemed all but over. An end of term, routine training session, however, heralded a new dawn when, unexpectedly, in the tunnel leading to the changing rooms at Central Park, Chris was taken to one side by coach, Eric Ashton:

Eric said to me 'Salford have come in for you and it could be a good move for you because there is a lot happening at that club. They've got this new chairman, Brian Snape, who looks like he is headed in the right direction.' All I knew about Salford at the time was that Griff Jenkins was there as their coach. Eric said 'Go and have a talk to them' which was basically saying 'Your days are numbered at Wigan.' Certainly they were with the board of directors! My first thought was I didn't want to go anywhere, but to cut a long story short, I met Mr Snape at his restaurant, the Ellesmere, on the East Lancashire Road, near Swinton, on Saturday 3 June 1967.

It was the first time I'd ever met him and I was a bit nervous, after all he was the club chairman and a very wealthy man. But he was a smashing bloke – as nice as pie – and I took to him right away. I think we had a cup of coffee each, and he told me he was going to make Salford into a very good rugby team. He didn't name names, which would have been unprofessional of him anyway, but told me 'We've got several other players that we're looking to bring in.' I didn't take a lot of persuading to be honest. Salford was not a big name then, but when I heard this man say with all sincerity what he was going to do, I was convinced, and I signed for him that night.

Looking back even now, I've not a bad word to say about Brian Snape, or his brother Keith Snape, who took over as chairman in 1978 when Brian moved to the Isle of Man. They did nothing but good as far as I was concerned. To be honest, all the time I knew him, I never called him Brian. Years later I used to go to the Premiership Trophy Final at Old Trafford. On one occasion, I was in the car park and saw my ex-Great Britain tour manager, Reg Parker, getting out of his car and with him he had Brian Snape. I walked over and I said 'Hello, Mr Snape.' He turned to Reg Parker and said 'He never would call me Brian!' It was just respect from my point of view.

The *Wigan Observer*, in its Friday, 9 June 1967 edition, under the headline 'Hesketh Goes To Salford', announced to its readers that Chris had moved on to Salford 'at a fee said to be in the region of £4,500.' Its writer further revealed that 'Although not on the official transfer list, Hesketh's name has been linked with possible moves to several clubs in the past year, notably Oldham, Warrington and Leigh. Wigan club secretary Ken Senior said this week: "Hesketh was not on the open to transfer list, but the Salford club approached the Wigan board about him and he agreed to go."' Chris obviously knew of Leigh's approach, but was unaware that Warrington and Oldham had made enquiries.

Meanwhile, the *Salford City Reporter*, on the same date, under the heading 'Salford Capture Two Internationals' went into overdrive. Its well-known sports journalist Tom Bergin wrote: 'The Salford Rugby Club shook the sporting world this week by signing two internationals – and both men have years of international football ahead of them. First of all on Saturday, in the comfortable surroundings of the Ellesmere Restaurant, the Reds completed the signing from Wigan of Chris Hesketh, then on Tuesday evening they added the Oldham forward, Charlie Bott, to their playing strength.' Bergin, who, from the 1920s, covered the affairs of the Salford club for over 50 years, had a further revelation. He went on to divulge that 'Hesketh comes a year later than might have been the case, for last summer Salford made a strong bid behind the scenes to secure him. At that time I spent hours checking his records and I was as disappointed as any when he remained at Central Park.' Again, it was an approach that Chris himself was blissfully unaware of.

The cause of Bergin's excitement at the double signing was not difficult to fathom. For years, the Salford team had been in the doldrums and the recruitment of international players had not been an option. Suddenly, within the space of a few days, the club had followed up the capture of Chris – an Under-24s cap – by acquiring, for a reported £4,000 fee, prop forward Bott, who had represented Great Britain against France in 1966.

The fact that Chris's former Wigan coach, Griff Jenkins was now at The Willows was more than mere coincidence. 'Griff Jenkins must have been influential in me going to Salford' says Chris. Jenkins had been in charge of team affairs at Salford since 1964, taking the team, ranked 29th in the League when he arrived, to a vastly improved 14th at the end of the 1966/67 term. Without any real stars in the side, he turned the club around under a regime that concentrated on improving the fitness level and commitment of his players:

Griff never raised his voice. He was what you would call a dour sort of fellah and wasn't a great conversationalist, but he'd come in to the changing room at half-time and be saying 'We need to do this and that, we need to get the ball wider', and so on. He was very meticulous and more focused on the science of rugby and the actual bones of the game, which I think had come from his time with that great Oldham team of the 1950s. I remember them coming to Central Park in November 1955 and beating Wigan 48-23.

He was into sprinting and speed. He was all for that and, of course, you could see what he did at Oldham. Training under Griff was hard but good, fitness was predominant. You've got to remember as well – unlike with the super fit lads of today – it was a time when we went to work every day. We had a pint now and again and some smoked. What impressed me about Griff was how he tried to replicate that great Oldham team as he went along. As far as I could see, he never had favourites or stars. But not many people did then. 'Star' is a very short word.

Quite often I travelled with him on the team coach. He was an old-fashioned sort of character and he was serious about rugby. Rugby league to Griff was everything. He used to run a pub with his wife in Leigh, and I used to go there sometimes. He was a nice man with not a bad bone in his body and he never did me any harm at all. He put the foundations in place at Salford and Cliff Evans and Les Bettinson, after that, built the rest.

Although the 1966/67 season was, effectively, over, Chris did not wait long before pulling on the club's famous red jersey. An end-of-season sevens tournament at Halifax, postponed from 28 May, when torrential rain washed it out, had been rescheduled for Sunday 11 June, the weekend after Chris had put pen to paper. He was pushed straight into a seven that lined up as: Bettinson,

Southward, Hesketh, McInnes, Whitehead, Burdell, Ogden.

Salford were paired with Oldham in the opening round and, despite leading 8-0 at the turn around, lost 10-8. Strangely, most Salford fans, not conditioned to seeing their team win sevens events – or anything else come to that – were pleased with the Reds showing, particularly that of Chris. Bergin's headline in the *Salford City Reporter*, which read 'Even In Defeat Reds Shine', echoed the general reaction and he went on to write 'The highlight was a magnificent long distance try by new signing Chris Hesketh, whose acceleration made it possible.'

I can remember playing in the Halifax Sevens because when I broke away, Oldham's Peter Smethurst chased me every yard of the way up the 'hill' at Thrum Hall. I thought once I'd got away I could jog because when you break in sevens you're normally gone. But I think he would have chased me if I'd run a hundred miles! Peter later became a very good team-mate.

It seemed that no sooner had the curtain come down on the season, than eminent *Manchester Evening News* rugby league correspondent, Jack McNamara – a New Zealander – was, just two months later, previewing the 1967/68 term. 'Salford are building up an imposing playing staff and there is now competition for every position. The signing of Chris Hesketh, in particular, should prove vital' predicted McNamara. His thoughts ahead of the opening match, a charity fixture at Wakefield Trinity, was, however, cautious. 'Salford must face their visit to Wakefield with trepidation. They got a walloping there in the top-16 play-off last season', reminding the Reds faithful of their teams 48-8 thrashing at Trinity's Belle Vue ground four months earlier in Salford's first Championship play-off match for 28 years. McNamara did conclude on a more optimistic note, however, adding that 'the signing of Hesketh, one of Wigan's most promising young centres, should prove a valuable capture, for speed and thrust in the centre has been sadly lacking in what is otherwise a well-balanced team.'

Although it was only a friendly, the result – 29-6 in Salford's favour – was a major upset, coming as it did against the current Champions, and elevated everyone's perception of what the Reds had to offer. Played on Saturday 11 August, the starting line-up for Chris's first 13-a-side match with his new colleagues read: Evans, Southward, Hesketh, Nestor, Murphy, McInnes, Brennan, Collier, Burdell, Bott, Whitehead, Argent, Hughes. One journalist recorded that: 'Salford approached this charity match like a cup-tie and were sharper and faster all round. Giant Wakefield Test centre Neil Fox was blotted out by Chris Hesketh, the close-season signing from Wigan.' The match also provided a debut for Bott:

Charlie Bott was a cracking buy. He never stopped working during a game – he worked and worked and worked. He'd give everything. He was a tackling machine. Charlie was a biggish lad – not in today's terms – but for then he was a big lad, and he had a lot of 'go-forward.' When you go on a team coach to an away match, you're sat there for what could be half an hour, two hours or three hours. Some players play cards, although I never did, and you'd have a laugh and a joke. I can remember talking to Charlie on the coach and being quite impressed by the fact that he was a metallurgist by profession. He was obviously a bright bloke who'd got a degree, but he didn't go into detail about his job. He emigrated to Australia in 1971, and I think he still lives there.

The first 'real' competitive match that Chris took part in for Salford was, ironically, at Central Park on Sunday 19 August, a match-up with Wigan in the opening round of the Lancashire Cup. Salford enjoyed unfamiliar treatment by the press ahead of the tie. Until recently a trip to Wigan was a definite 'no-no' for the club but now they were being hailed as possible winners. One prediction said 'The new slim-line Frank Collier, who reserves extra energy for his Wigan appearances, and centre Chris Hesketh, whose true worth never seems to have been appreciated at Central Park, could be two of the men to sink Wigan.' Salford's robust prop forward Collier had left Wigan in 1964, having played well over 300 games in almost 13 years with the Cherry and Whites, joining Widnes and becoming a Challenge Cup winner with them at Wembley the same year:

He was at Wigan when I went as a kid to watch them play. I always looked up at him. In fact, everybody looked up at Frank Collier because he was so big anyway! But he was always a rum bugger. People would say to him 'Frank can you not take this game serious!' but that's how he was. He'd be having a laugh going up the tunnel leading to the pitch before the match. One referee, who sent him off, said to him 'What's your name?' and he gave another name! He was a good man in the dressing room. There can be people who never speak because they're nervous or just quiet. Some keep talking and Frank was like that.

Apart from the fact Salford had shocked Wakefield in the Red Rose Cup charity game the previous week, their pre-match backing was also based on them upsetting the odds by winning 18-6 at Central Park the previous March in a second round Challenge Cup tie. It was the club's first win at Wigan since 1938, ending a run of 27 defeats. Chris himself had been on the Wigan wing that day. 'Salford played very well and hammered us. Alan McInnes had a good game at stand-off for Salford and I remember Terry Ogden playing very well in the front row. Both were future team-mates of mine at Salford.' Salford did not let the forecasters down in the Lancashire Cup tie registering an 18-14 victory. The Reds flying winger Paul Murphy – a former rugby union player with Preston Grasshoppers who was to marry Brian Snape's daughter –

provided the highlights for the away fans as he flew into the corner for two second half tries in as many minutes, the second off a pass from Chris:

It was a strange feeling going into the visitors dressing room because, of course, I'd always gone into the Wigan one. I can imagine what Phil Neville must have felt like when he went back to Old Trafford with Everton in 2005 after all those years as a Manchester United player. I bet he nearly walked into the home dressing room! And then I was on that Central Park field again, less than 500 yards away from where I was born. I suppose many players feel the same when they move away. But you get over it. It's only a game of rugby.

Having played his first three matches for Salford in the centre, Chris was moved to stand-off for the trip to Castleford on 25 August, replacing an out-of-form McInnes. Although Chris 'did a tremendous amount of tackling' it was not enough to avert a 21-14 defeat. Three days later he was back in the centre for Salford's first home match of the campaign, beating local rivals Swinton 17-8 in front of a crowd just below the 10,000 mark. The visitors had home supporters feeling nervous by half-time through building up an 8-2 lead, Chris launching the comeback when he 'corkscrewed over for a try' which, apart from the Halifax Sevens, was his first for the club. It was on the strength of his performance against Swinton, that the county selectors picked him for his Lancashire debut. Incredibly, his recognition had come within a month of his first Salford appearance:

I went straight into the first team at Salford and I was picked for Lancashire probably because I was playing regularly. Salford was very much a friendly club and I soon settled and it gave me confidence. I wouldn't say that it wasn't strict at Salford but they didn't really go 'bananas' at you if you did something wrong. We played a lot of home matches on Friday night and, of course, we had this wonderful club house – the Willows Variety Centre – which married you into things overall. Visiting players would go in there after the match and be really impressed. Even now it's still a wonderful place to go. You could see it was a rugby club that wanted to go places.

His induction to the Lancashire team took place on 12 September, a Tuesday evening trip to Workington's Derwent Park for a tough looking inter-county baptism against Cumberland. Chris played centre to Barrow's talented and elusive wingman, Bill Burgess, who claimed two of the tries as Lancashire won comfortably enough 19-6. The appearance also earned Chris an early bonus, as his contract with Salford contained the addendum that he would receive £250 'if he attains county honours', and there was another £250 waiting to be handed over 'should he gain (full) international honours.' Also earning his county debut was Salford hooker Bob Burdell, a former Liverpool City player, who joined the Reds as a bargain-buy from St Helens 12 months earlier and quickly won over the hearts of the Willows crowd with his energetic non-stop displays in the loose. The Lancashire line-up was: Barrow (St Helens), Burgess (Barrow), Hesketh (Salford), Myler (St Helens), Glover (Warrington), Aspinall (Warrington), Bishop (St Helens), Halsall (St Helens), Burdell (Salford), Brady (Warrington), Sanderson (Barrow), Parr (Warrington), Clarke (Warrington). Substitutes: Tees (Barrow), Laughton (Wigan):

I thought very highly of playing for my county, I thought it was fantastic! But Workington is always a tough place to go, there is something about it. It is the kind of place where, to be honest, you felt slightly intimidated. As players, we used to have a laugh about it because, whether I was there with Lancashire or Salford, we used to say how big the Cumbrians were! The coat-hangers always seemed to be a foot higher than in any other dressing room! That was probably just to put you off! And I remember it said on the wall in the showers 'plas (please) turn tap off.'

I wasn't with Bob Burdell at Salford that long because he joined Wigan at the start of 1970 and played for them at Wembley that year. He lived at Southport, which was a bit of a trek getting to Salford because there was no motorway then. He was a very popular player and it was common knowledge that he wore a wig as he was a bit thin on top. Jackie Brennan and one or two others used to have him on unmercifully about it. He'd be in the players' bath and somebody would throw his wig in and everyone thought it was a rat or something and you'd see all these lads shoot out. But that's the sort of guys they were!

Just four days before the county game, Chris had travelled to Halifax with the Reds for a Friday evening fixture. Disappointingly, Salford lost the match 27-18, having led 7-6 at the break. More significant for the travelling supporters, however, was the eleventh hour debut of Peter Smethurst, who, during his three years at the club, became one of the Salford fans' most loved players. A former three-quarter with Swinton, he had moved to Oldham six years earlier, establishing himself as one of the best uncapped second-row forwards around. Signed earlier that day for £3,250, he was brought straight into the Salford starting thirteen at loose forward:

Peter was a cracking bloke, outgoing but very professional. He was proud of his fitness and was a dedicated trainer. He wasn't a drinker – he'd have the odd bottle of beer – and never smoked. If somebody smacked him he'd get up and he'd look them in the eye and just smile! He was super fit and super strong and he did very well for himself. He joined

Leigh and won a medal with them at Wembley in 1971. He used to be a window cleaner in Swinton before he got his butcher's shop in Roe Green, Worsley.

The signing of Smethurst was all part of the pledge Snape made to Chris on their first meeting. He was the first significant signing since the arrival of Bott and himself but more were in the offing. 'You didn't need to be clever to see that a lot of the players we did have weren't, if you like, of the Wigan–St Helens quality, and probably I wasn't as well' says Chris, 'but what Brian Snape did do was he signed Bob Prosser, he signed David Watkins, he signed Colin Dixon, and he signed a good few others as well.'

Chris, himself, had been given credit by McNamara in his *Manchester Evening News* column as having 'steadied up the three-quarters' in the opening weeks although, despite his impressing the county selectors, also offered the opinion that Chris 'has been comparatively quiet since he moved from Wigan, but he is an unobtrusive type of footballer who does much valuable work.' There may well have been an element of truth in McNamara's words but, as the season rumbled on and Chris became adjusted to playing with his new colleagues, he started to receive rave reviews from all quarters well before the end of the campaign.

His second appearance for Lancashire was on 11 October, a Wednesday evening game against the Australian tourists at The Willows. The Aussies won 14-2, one of their tries coming from legendary centre Reg Gasnier who formed a formidable right flank with wingman Ken Irvine. 'Gasnier was quick but Irvine was like lightning' recalls Chris.

The following Tuesday, 17 October, Chris burst into try-scoring form as he treated the Weaste crowd to his first Salford hat-trick, providing the highlights in a 23-7 win over Whitehaven. Inevitably, it earned him the man of the match award, dominating the back-pages the next day with headlines like 'Hat-Trick Hesketh The Star', 'Hesketh Takes The Honours' and 'Hesketh Lifts Gloom.'

Apart from Hesketh's trio, another significant event that took place that evening was the signing of scrum-half Bob Prosser from St Helens for £2,000. Prosser – who was at half-back when Chris made his Great Britain Under-24s debut – had joined the Saints two years earlier from Newport Rugby Union Club but had been unable to separate the in-form Tommy Bishop from his first team jersey. The signing was noteworthy because Salford had been pursuing the signature of the Wales Rugby Union captain David Watkins, Prosser's former half-back partner at Newport. One newspaper – unkindly towards Prosser perhaps – suggested that the Reds had 'bought a sprat to catch a mackerel.' Whatever the motive – and Prosser certainly provided valuable cover for team captain Brennan – Watkins signed two days later. Watkins' debut, against Oldham at The Willows the next day, pulled in over 10,000 excited fans, the largest so far that season, Salford winning 12-6, the Welshman giving the media plenty of copy through covering 70 yards for a try and landing two drop-goals:

I got on very well indeed with David. But it wasn't like Chris Hesketh or Charlie Bott coming to Salford, you were getting a bloke who'd recently been on a New Zealand tour with the British Lions rugby union team and that was almost equivalent in football terms to buying a player who'd just won the World Cup with Germany. He caught the public imagination because he had that lovely Welsh accent and he was dapper – he dressed very modern and, of course, he had an E-type Jag! But he also had everything he needed on the rugby pitch. He was lightning and faster than anybody I'd ever seen from stood still to flat out. It was like a stride and a half. Now that's pretty good going! David was a wonderful player and you'd always have him in your side. Some people used to say he couldn't tackle, and there were comments like 'hit him with your wallet!' That was a little bit unfair because you can't have everything and you can't do everything. You've got to remember if myself, Kenny Gill or Paul Charlton could work an overlap, and he was on the end of it, he was over for a try, he was that quick. If you could get that ball to him a yard away from anybody else he'd go and score for you.

I was what I call a basic rugby player. I used to run and tackle and do everything right but I never had the electric pace that Watkins had. Don't get me wrong – I was quick. I was quick enough to play for Great Britain, so that wasn't bad, but there are certain people that have got extra and Watkins was one of them. Because of the amount of money he got to sign for Salford, which, at the time, was a fortune to all the other lads, there was always someone who'd go out of their way to try and 'do' him. You'd think 'Hold on a bit, this game's hard enough without that.' Playing to the rules is tough enough. When you start going outside the rules you should really be walking down the tunnel back to the dressing room.

His kicking in general play was a big bonus, and he became a very reliable goal kicker as well. He was also brilliant at scoring from drop-goal attempts. I remember in one match at Salford, we were playing towards the club end and it was coming up to half-time. We had the ball and there was one or two tackle left, and he was about 45 or 50 yards out and just dropped a goal! Rather than just take a few more tackles in, we're winning 10-0, so we might as well be 12-0 up.

The Salford team was growing in confidence and, having pulled off a shock 8-3 Challenge Cup replay win at St Helens the previous February, thereby eliminating the cup holders, they repeated their success in a League fixture at Knowsley Road on 24 November. The Reds led only 5-4 at the break and were under threat during the second half. Billy Benyon broke away with the great winger Tom van Vollenhoven creating the overlap on the outside. A certain score was averted when Chris reacted quickly enough to knock the ball down as it sped towards the South African flyer. A penalty goal increased the Salford lead to 7-4, Chris then intercepting a pass to race 40 yards, deep into St Helens territory, before transferring to his winger Peter Crank. Watkins supported to take the ball and, on the turn and under pressure, was just wide with a drop-kick. Despite that failure it was a passage of play that restored Salford's confidence, there being no further scoring, the Reds claiming the only try of the match. It was the third victory of a 12-match winning sequence but, more significant was that it established Salford's credentials as a leading contender for future honours.

It was during that 12-game run that Chris suffered the first serious injury of his career when he fractured his forearm against Barrow at The Willows on 19 January. 'Billy Burgess broke it!' reflects Chris. 'They kicked through and I ran back and was dropping on the ball. He lashed out and broke it then.' His arm was put in plaster but, undeterred, he immediately began light training with the intention of returning to the fold in time for the second round of the Challenge Cup, scheduled for the last weekend in February. Salford had high hopes of doing well in the competition but Chris never made it back as quickly as anticipated. Salford never made it to Wembley either, failing to get beyond the second stage when eventual finalists Wakefield Trinity eliminated the Reds by 8-4 at The Willows, watched by 14,000.

Having missed nine matches – plus Lancashire's victory over Yorkshire at Widnes on 24 January which clinched the county championship for the Red Rose – Chris returned on 29 March when Wigan visited. In an exciting contest, seen by over 11,800 fans and described by Bergin in the *Salford City Reporter* as a game that 'would have made a good cup final', Chris shook off 10 weeks of frustration and comparative inactivity by taking the man of the match award against his former club. The Reds won 15-13, Chris having a new wing partner in 21-year-old Mike Kelly, who had signed from Bradford Northern before the Challenge Cup deadline in late January for £3,500. At the same time, the Reds had splashed out a further £4,000 to secure the giant Welsh prop Jim Mills from Halifax. Mills never really settled at The Willows and went on to achieve greater fame, and notoriety, during a rewarding career with Widnes.

Another event Chris missed during his lay-off – and was probably glad to! – was a friendly against the full Great Britain side, who were preparing for the 1968 World Cup, to be held in Australia and New Zealand at the end of the season. The game took place at The Willows on 5 February, on a freezing cold Monday evening during a snowstorm. It was abandoned after 35 minutes – much to the relief of the dithering participants and most of the 4,500 attendance. A rematch was organised for 5 April, the second game in Chris's comeback. This time the weather was kinder, and 6,000 rolled up to see Britain win 20-5. Salford's only touchdown came in the dying seconds before half-time when 'Watkins came through the opposition like a flash of lightning from his own 25 before kicking deep, and eventually Hesketh dived on the bobbling ball for a great try.'

Salford ended the League campaign in ninth position – a climb of five places from the previous year – but lost rather ignominiously at Castleford in the opening round of the top 16 Championship play-off by 47-15. It brought an abrupt end to the official element of the season but, with the Salford club continuing to demonstrate initiative, there were still a few more commitments for Chris and his colleagues.

On 28 May, the Salford team and officials set off by coach on a two-match 'propaganda' tour. The problem was that the first match was in Scotland and the second in South Wales. 'It was just an arduous long drag' recalls Chris. 'It was a coach trip all the way up to Scotland. An overnight stay in Hawick, then the match obviously, followed by another overnight stay. Then, the following day, taking the coach down to Abertillery.' The first game on 29

May, a Wednesday evening, was against Hull Kingston Rovers at Bridgend Park, Jedburgh. The Rovers won 36-33 and Chris, along with Watkins – the pair being considered 'star' attractions – were 'subbed to save them for the second match.' The match in Abertillery took place on Saturday, 1 June, this time with Bradford Northern providing the opposition. The obvious interest for the Welsh crowd was the appearance of Watkins in the Salford side with former Wales rugby union international full-back Terry Price in Northern's line-up. The Yorkshire side took the honours 46-22 in a match watched by 11,500, considerably more than the reported 1,000 that turned out in Scotland. 'They were games that were supposed to promote rugby league in the strongest bastions of rugby union that you could ever come across' says Chris. 'Whether it did any good, or not, I don't know, although I believe rugby league in Wales these days is quite flourishing. But union is a worldwide game, so I don't think it will be in my lifetime that rugby league takes over.'

Probably the most memorable feature of the summer of '68, though, was the club's unexpected and unprecedented dominance in sevens rugby. They were invited to compete in four tournaments, at Huddersfield, Leeds and Halifax during May, and Wigan's annual pre-season event in early August, winning the lot. The Salford seven was virtually the same each time: Kelly (Bettinson replaced him at Wigan due to a broken collar-bone), Hesketh, Watkins, Prosser, Whitehead, Brennan (Burdell played in the first at Huddersfield) and Doug Hill. Of the 56 tries scored in the four events, Chris was the joint leading try scorer with Kelly, claiming 11 apiece, whilst Watkins contributed 10. Not only did Chris score some 'scintillating tries' – as one journalist described it – but his defence was also a key element in the wide, open spaces that inevitably favoured the team in possession:

> I've got to say that David (Watkins) was more or less the authority on sevens and we all knew that. David was a sevens

expert, whether it be union or league. His expertise was union, obviously, but he brought it to league and he knew when to have a breather. He'd say 'Come on, we're ten points in front, let's slow it down.' And as soon as somebody tried to tackle you – two of them sometimes – you'd get rid of the ball, and you knew it was a try. I could always beat the first man and if I'd got Mike Kelly – and, in later years, Keith Fielding – on one side and Watkins on the other, a try was nearly always the result. We'd be on the field at Headingley, for example, and someone would say 'I'll run at him, sidestep and then give you the ball' because the gaps were that wide. And remember, when we first won those sevens, every time you scored you got the ball back from the restart because they kicked off again. Eventually they changed the rules because of us. It was daft anyway when you think about it.

I don't remember each individual sevens, but I do remember that, all of a sudden, because we had David and a pretty quick three in the pack as well, we were very difficult to play against. Dougie (Hill) was a former union man from the Midlands who we had signed earlier in the season from St Helens. He could hold the ball with one hand and was a cracking sevens player. Bob Prosser had played sevens with David at Newport and was a great passer of the ball. He wasn't a sidestepper, he ran more in a straight line but he was very quick. Mike Kelly was a Huddersfield lad and, although he wasn't blistering, he was very fast, whilst Jackie (Brennan) was very effective at blocking up that middle.

Early on, we hammered some teams but, eventually, they picked it up over the years. But it was very entertaining for the fans and I remember most of it was played on good dry Saturdays or Sundays. We had some very enjoyable times. We've got more winners' tankards, David and myself, than we know what to do with!

4

WEMBLEY REVISTED

Wembley Stadium and the Challenge Cup Final is an occasion that every rugby league player wants to savour and, for most clubs and their supporters, it is, unquestionably, their 'Holy Grail.' Chris had already sampled its unique atmosphere with Wigan in 1966 but, frustratingly, was not called off the bench to tread its famous lush turf. In 1969, he got a second chance, and this time he was very much in the thick of the action. As Chris, himself, says, 'Wembley was the place you wanted to go and watch your team as a supporter or, if you were lucky enough, to play there yourself. They are few and far between, the people who did that.'

It came at the climax of only his second season at Salford. Chris had continued to impress and progress throughout the 1968/69 term whilst, at the same time and with the support of Brian Snape's cheque book, the team was growing increasingly stronger. The campaign had opened with a slight hiccup for 23-year-old Chris when, having been named for a side labelled the Salford Reds, effectively the first team, against the Salford Yellows – the 'A' team – in the pre-season public trial match on 9 August, he had to pull out. The reason was to visit a specialist for an examination on a troublesome knee. Happily, the diagnosis showed it was not as serious as first thought, and he was able to take up his usual centre berth in the team for the trip to Bradford Northern the following Wednesday, 14 August. Salford won 11-5, future club coach Les Bettinson being Chris's winger on that occasion.

One of his biggest disappointments to date in the quest for honours occurred at The Willows on 9 October. Having comfortably eliminated Warrington and Whitehaven in the opening rounds, Salford faced a routine-looking home Lancashire Cup semi-final against mid-table Oldham. A crowd of 12,000 passed through the turnstiles for the Wednesday evening clash, most of them with the expectancy of seeing the Red Devils reach their first major final since 1939. Oldham had other ideas, winning 12-9 to become eventual runners-up to St Helens. According to *Manchester Evening News* writer Brian Bearshaw 'Chris Hesketh alone looked to have the penetration to worry Oldham.' With David Watkins – who took over the captaincy from scrum-half Jackie Brennan during the season – unavailable due to a rib injury, Brennan had relocated to the stand-off slot with Bob Prosser at scrum-half. The reverberation following the defeat brought about a swift change for the League fixture at Whitehaven three days later. Chris took over the number six jersey, with Brennan feeding the scrum. Salford won 21-2, and Chris, as one writer put it, 'had a field day in the out-half spot.' Having proved his versatility yet again, he was back at centre the following week, Watkins returning to reclaim his place.

The fine form Chris was enjoying ensured he retained his slot for both of Lancashire's inter-county fixtures, scoring their only try in the 10-5 defeat by Yorkshire at Craven Park, Hull, on 25 September, a reverse that ultimately took the county title east of the Pennines. His second appearance, against Cumberland on Wednesday 6 November at Knowsley Road, St Helens, began a hectic spell for Chris of three matches in three days – and for three different teams! The day after the county match – a 24-19 win for Lancashire – he was a late inclusion for England's meeting with Wales at The Willows. His centre partner in the Lancashire side, Hull's Dick Gemmell, was originally selected but sustained an injury at Knowsley Road and Chris, on 'stand-by', took his place.

In what was Chris's senior international debut – won 24-17 by Wales – the England team was: Jefferson (Keighley), Smith (Leeds), Benyon (St Helens), Hesketh (Salford), Atkinson (Leeds),

Davies (Swinton), Shoebottom (Leeds), Hartley (Castleford), Taylor (Oldham), Watson (St Helens), Morgan (Featherstone Rovers), Parr (Warrington), Batten (Leeds). Substitutes: Buckley (Swinton), Robinson (Swinton). The appearance increased Chris's bank account by a further £250, as stipulated in his contract with Salford.

His trilogy of matches was completed, with Salford, on 8 November, a Friday evening fixture, again at The Willows, visitors Workington Town winning 18-10. Chris, quoted at the time as saying 'I was absolutely shattered after the Workington match', recalls 'I had three games in three days and went to work full time as well! Do you know what? I honestly don't remember even thinking about it at the time. You can't really save yourself if you're playing for your country or your county, you've got to go flat out.'

One player who did impress in the home defeat to Workington was Salford's newest recruit, former England rugby union forward Mike Coulman, making only his fourth appearance, and 'whose running', according to Bearshaw in the *Manchester Evening News*, 'was hearty and fearless.' Signed towards the end of September from the Birmingham-based Moseley Rugby Union Club, he was the first of three high-profile signings made by the club during the autumn, the others being Great Britain internationals Bill Burgess and Colin Dixon:

> I've always got on very well with Mike Coulman. One thing about Mike was that he was big, he was strong and he was fit and, for a bloke of his size, he was very quick. Mike was an ex-union man, but he very soon impressed me. He learned and he improved. I think a lot of that was down to Cliff Evans when he became coach. I remember Cliff would be telling him to run into the gap. Kenny Gill used to say 'I'll put the ball in that gap. You just make sure you get there.' He was extremely robust but he wasn't dirty. Other players seemed to clout him simply, I think, because he was so big. I think Mike was underrated. People used to have a go at him,

saying he was lazy. But I'd say 'What do you mean? He's just run 60 yards with that ball.' Because he was so big it might take him a little longer to recover.

Salford fans were treated to an early Christmas present by the club on 19 December with the sensational double signing of Barrow winger Burgess for £6,000 and Halifax back-row forward Dixon in exchange for Mike Kelly and £11, 500 – a rugby league record. Salford rated Burgess so highly that a month earlier, when Barrow visited The Willows on 22 November, they assigned Chris to the wing specifically to snuff out the danger he posed. Dixon, a former rugby union prodigy, had joined Halifax as a three-quarter in 1961 from the Cardiff International Athletic Club, and had been a Salford target for some time. The previous May, the Yorkshire club had rejected a bid from the Snape coffers of £6,000, plus Jim Mills. The pair made their debuts in the home match with Wakefield Trinity, the day after being signed:

Billy Burgess was, in my eyes, one of the best pure wingers I've ever seen. He was brilliant. I've never seen anybody drift past people like him. He could go by defenders and you'd think 'How did he get past them then?' He was a lovely man as well, very modest, almost shy really. We played at Whitehaven during November 1969, and the rain was absolutely hammering down – it was one of those days. It was a very tough match. We were playing uphill and the mud was deep. All of a sudden, Billy got the ball from 75 yards out. It looked like his feet weren't touching the floor whilst mine were going down six inches every time! Billy was just flying up that wing and basically it was a winning try – he ghosted over and we won 13-7. Unfortunately, he was very injury prone after he came to Salford. His shoulder kept coming out. I remember, in a Challenge Cup match in February 1970, he scored a try in the top right hand corner at

Featherstone. When he put the ball down his shoulder came out. He was never the same and had to retire shortly afterwards.

Colin Dixon was a class act. He was a very special player. When he started as a centre he was quick and big and he developed into a powerful second row forward. He was slippery to get hold of and he was hard and strong. You run out of words for describing Colin really.

On 27 January, Salford travelled to the Boulevard to meet Hull, always a tricky assignment at the best of times. Due to incessant rain ahead of the match, the pitch was very muddy and it was decided to play Chris at stand-off for the second time that season, leaving the more lightweight Watkins on the bench. A surprise was the decision to put two second-row forwards, Stuart Whitehead and Dixon, in the centre, in an effort to combat a tough looking home thirteen in the heavy conditions. So successful was Whitehead in his new role that he was retained there as Chris's co-centre for the remainder of the season. Salford drew the match 5-5 with one headline declaring 'Hesketh Turns On Star Show.' The writer went on to say that 'Salford played the better football on a heavy, muddy pitch and their outstanding player was centre Chris Hesketh who switched to stand-off and gained the man-of-the-match award, making the try for Terry Ogden.' Other reports said 'he was the only player able to make any real progress' and 'the only player who made any really decisive runs in the treacherous mud', proving, yet again, what an asset Chris was to the club in whatever position they chose to play him in.

An unusual diversion during the season was the staging, for the first and only time, of a National Sevens competition. It was an idea no doubt inspired by Salford's revolutionary approach to the miniature form of rugby, as evidenced by their outstanding success the previous summer. The final stages, shown live on BBC television, took place at Station Road, Swinton, on Thursday 6

February, in the most terrible weather imaginable. On a freezing evening and with snow falling heavily, Workington Town pulled off a shock, winning 10-5 in the deciding match. For Chris, it was a disastrous evening in more ways than one. 'Somebody stood on my hip' he recalls. 'I was tackling someone and I landed on the side of their boot and it cut me so deeply it curled the skin back. I remember it because it hurt so much.'

Happier times lay ahead, with Salford reaching Wembley for the first time since 1939. The Reds had won an emotion-charged quarter-final against Widnes 20-7, watched by a crowd of 18,825 that, somehow, had managed to squeeze into The Willows. In completing what was described as 'the finest move of the match', Chris claimed the last of Salford's four tries following up a kick-through by his winger Paul Jackson. Carried away by the euphoria of the moment, Chris tempted fate after the match by telling the *Daily Mirror's* Joe Humphreys that 'Another 80 minutes and we shall be at Wembley.' Warrington, their semi-final opponents, no doubt had other ideas!

The most important game of Chris's career, to date, was to take place on familiar territory, Central Park providing the venue on Saturday 22 March. Whether it was the occasion itself, with Wembley awaiting the winners, but Salford were jittery for much of the first half, whereas Warrington looked sharper and more determined. Jack Nott, writing in the *News of the World*, said: 'Astute kicking by Watkins and interceptions by Hesketh and Burgess did much to relieve early tension on the Salford line.' With five minutes to go before half-time, the only try had gone to Warrington, scored by former Salford loose-forward Arthur Hughes. Fortunately, Salford's own number 13, Welshman Ron Hill – signed from Castleford four months earlier – was on target with two penalties to give his team a narrow 4-3 lead. It was at that point that Salford, inspired by a break from Chris, utilised their extra pace. Jack McNamara noted in the *Manchester Evening News*: 'Hesketh made the opening as he stood and wove and sent an opponent racing the wrong way. Whitehead took up the pass, drew the remaining defender, and sent Paul Jackson in at the corner.' Hill missed the difficult conversion but added a vital penalty in the last seconds for a 9-3 interval cushion. Salford added two more tries through Whitehead and Burgess in the second half, eventually winning 15-8. Chris, according to Bergin in the *Salford City Reporter*, had played his part, having 'completely stitched up the centre with his solid play.' All three of the Reds tries had involved Whitehead, who had his finest hour in a Salford jersey. 'He had a brilliant game' says Chris. 'Stuart was a very good second-row forward and he was a good centre. He probably lacked a bit of pace for a centre but he had a great game that day.'

Whether it was from an adrenalin rush brought about by reaching Wembley, where there opponents would be Castleford, but the Salford team was on a roll, suffering just one defeat in 21 matches. Over the Easter period they won four matches in style. On the Tuesday (1 April) leading up to the holiday weekend, they beat visitors Widnes 29-3, Chris sidestepping his way over the line to register the first of his sides seven tries. A 49-7 win at Blackpool Borough on Good Friday was followed the next day by a 19-3 success in the derby match with Swinton at Station Road. Chris, who scored the last of the Reds' three tries off a Brennan pass, won the man of the match award, one journalist declaring: 'He deserved it for his cover-tackling alone, at least twice preventing almost certain tries.' Most satisfying for Chris was probably the 37-5 verdict over Wigan at The Willows on Easter Monday watched by 15,300. In the *Daily Mail*, Brian Batty wrote: 'Centre Hesketh, sold by Wigan last season, staggered his former club by taking Dixon's pass and cutting through brilliantly for Salford's first try.' His coach Griff Jenkins went even further, saying later: 'Hesketh has a fair turn of pace and when we walloped Wigan at home on Easter Monday he made Eric Ashton and Colin Tyrer look a couple of slouches when he scored. There was a lot of good tries in that match but that was the best for me.'

Ashton's last appearance of an illustrious career for Wigan followed a month later in the Championship play-off. Salford travelled to Central Park with a semi-final place awaiting the victors. In front of over 16,600 spectators, Wigan went 10-3 up early in the match but, by half-time, Salford had gained the initiative to lead 11-10. Helped by three magical touchdowns from Burgess and a match-clinching try from Smethurst, who raced under the posts from the halfway line nine minutes from time, the Reds went on to win 26-21. Phil King, in *The People*, described it as: 'The most exciting game I've seen all season!' McNamara said: 'When all seemed lost in the early stages, Salford owed an irredeemable debt to the courageous tackling of centre Chris Hesketh and full-back Ken Gwilliam.' Chris recalls 'Peter Smethurst had an absolute blinder that day. It was almost as if the Salford team had come of age then.' Unfortunately, the bubble burst the following week at Headingley, Leeds winning the semi-final 22-12. Salford had come close, being 12-6 ahead at half-time and trailing by only 14-12 with four minutes left to play.

Two days later, on Monday 12 May, Salford put that setback behind them as they boarded a coach to Blackpool at the start of 'Wembley Week.' Their destination was the Stuart Hotel, situated at the South Shore end of the popular resort. 'It was owned by Brian Snape' remembers Chris. Arrangements had been made with Blackpool Football Club to train at their Bloomfield Road ground, the first day being concluded by a visit to the local cinema to help unwind.

There was concern in the camp for Chris during the Tuesday training session, when he had to break off for treatment. The report at the time said that Chris 'had strained a calf muscle, but later resumed training, although he ran warily.' Coach Jenkins was quoted as saying 'He'll be all right. It was just reaction after a sauna bath last night.' When Wednesday arrived, Jenkins was proved correct, the press announcing to relieved Salford fans that Chris had recovered following treatment. Looking back at it now, Chris cannot specifically remember the incident, his only comment being 'How do you get a reaction to having a sauna?'

After three days and nights by the seaside, it was time for a change of venue and the squad travelled south by train on Thursday morning to stay at the splendid Oatlands Park Hotel, situated in Weybridge. Set in its own grounds, complete with a nine-hole golf course, it was a popular base for the Scotland rugby union squad whenever they were due at Twickenham to take on England, and Manchester City had stayed there three weeks earlier prior to their 1-0 FA Cup Final win over Leicester City. After the train arrived in London during the afternoon, the party made a detour to visit Wembley Stadium before continuing to their Surrey destination

One surprising piece of information was that the Oatlands was then regarded as a 'temperance' hotel. Chris, himself, was quoted in the *Daily Mirror* as saying 'We must be the driest rugby league team ever to go to Wembley. We were asked to cut out the drinks until after Wembley and I am certainly feeling fitter for it. But if any player wants the odd one there is no objection.'

The emotion attached to an appearance at Wembley was probably felt most strongly by three of the teams elder statesmen; Jackie Brennan, Martin Dickens and Peter Smethurst. All of them had turned 30 and none had appeared in a Challenge Cup Final before. Brennan – a Wigan lad – had been at the club for ten years, having signed from Blackpool Borough in 1959:

> You could write another book about Jackie Brennan. Jackie is a cracking bloke, a wonderful scrum-half with the finest dummy pass I've ever seen in my life. He'd get all the defence to go one way and he'd just walk under the sticks and put it down. He was a deceptively strong man and he also played at loose forward towards the end of his career. He didn't get many representative honours because he played in an era when you had a lot of really good half-backs around. The thing about Jackie was he had no airs and graces. I

remember us all going down Wembley Way towards the
stadium in the coach, then getting off the coach and walking
into the dressing room and thinking 'Blimey!' To me, it was
an awesome feeling, but Jackie seemed very relaxed.

In the traditional pre-match stroll around the playing area,
resplendent in their club blazers, Chris, along with Dickens and
Gwilliam, spotted a crowd of Salford supporters at the front of the
stands and sauntered across to say 'Hello' and sign autographs. 'The
pitch at Wembley was a long way from the crowd, with the track
around it' says Chris, 'But you knew where the Salford end was before
the match. You could see the mass of red and you could hear the
overall shouting, but you couldn't hear individuals. It was just so big.'

Salford selected the following team: Gwilliam, Burgess,
Whitehead, Hesketh, Jackson, Watkins, Brennan, Ogden, Dickens,
Bott, Coulman, Dixon, R Hill. Substitutes: Prosser, Smethurst.
The match itself got off to the worst possible start for Salford. As
Watkins kicked off to the right of the field, Burgess – thought by
many to be the Reds' biggest attacking threat – was following up
the kick when he was blatantly laid out off the ball. Although
Eddie Waring, in his BBC commentary declared 'Already there's a
man flat out on the turf', it was unseen, apparently, by any of the
officials. 'I remember the kick-off' says Chris, 'and then "Bang!" It
possibly ruined the game for us really because the incident
reverberated across the field.' Either way, Burgess, who was
heavily concussed, became a passenger for much of the final.

In a tense, unspectacular opening, the only score was a Salford
penalty by Hill in the third minute until, eight minutes before half-
time, the first try went to Castleford. Taking the ball from a scrum
near the Salford line, Castleford skipper and stand-off Alan
Hardisty transferred to centre Keith Howe who scored in the right
corner. Chris just failed to halt Howe's progress when, as one
writer put it, the Castleford man was 'brought to his knees by
Hesketh's despairing ankle grab, (but) he was on the move again in

an instant.' With the match being played out through a combination of sunshine and showers, Chris had lost his footing on the saturated grass whilst making the tackle. 'I did slip' says Chris, 'but when I went down underneath him, I should have put him down.' Chris, clearly disappointed with himself and completely out of character, kicked the ball away in disgust!

Another Hill penalty put Salford 4-3 ahead, when, three minutes before the interval, one of the game's biggest talking points took place after Chris had exploded through the Castleford defence from 30 yards out. Whilst Castleford had anticipated a pass to the right towards midfield, Dickens, at acting half-back, spun the ball in the opposite direction to Chris, who took off down the left hand channel. He beat five defenders on a mesmerising run to the left corner flag, described by Jack Nott as a 'remarkable slice of solo play, (as) he weaved and wormed his way through the defensive network.' According to the officials, however, he grounded the ball in the corner just inches short, although video footage of the match seems to indicate Chris slid over the line. As the Salford fans celebrated, referee Deryk Brown awarded Castleford a penalty for a double-movement by Chris. Chris told one journalist 'I swear I was over the line' and still refutes the decision today:

Was it given as a double movement? Is that what he said? I can actually remember the incident and I can visualise myself scoring if you know what I mean. As far as I was concerned, the referee looked at the touch judge, who said 'He's short' in which case we should have played on. As far as I was concerned the ball was on the line and on the line is a try. I'll be very, very surprised if I made a double movement. I was expecting to get up and it was a try, and probably we'd have gone on to win then. I was told the touch judge disallowed it.

Thirteen minutes into the second half, Castleford regained the lead at 8-4 through a converted try from Alan Hardisty. The Yorkshire side's tails were well and truly up at this point and Chris stopped a certain try when wrapping up winger Alan Lowndes with a head-on tackle. A third Hill penalty halved the arrears before Castleford had the final say with a Keith Hepworth try just before full-time.

Having collected their losers' medals, Salford trudged dejectedly and despairingly back to their dressing room. 'There was so much expectancy from the Salford "speccies" you felt like you let them down' says Chris. But at least he could hold his head high, the press being almost unanimous in naming him and Dixon as the two outstanding performers in the Reds camp. Bentley wrote: 'Salford's three-quarter line never got going. Flying wingman Bill Burgess was almost as much a spectator as I was, and only centre Chris Hesketh ever looked likely to fool Castleford's great defence.' Bergin: '(In addition to Dixon) Hesketh was the other great Salford success and to my mind was the team's best player, for he gave a non-stop display on attack and defence, first on one wing and then on the other.' Humphreys: 'Salford were not incisive; Chris Hesketh and Colin Dixon apart, no one had the thrust to suggest they would score a try.' McNamara: 'Centre Chris Hesketh was easily Salford's most dangerous attacking back.' Although 21-year-old Malcolm Reilly deservedly won the Lance Todd Trophy as man of the match with Dixon runner-up, two of the journalists present gave their vote as the outstanding player to Chris:

You've got to remember, Castleford were a much more experienced rugby league team than we were. We were brand new. They had a hell of a good pack. Once they got in front – and we weren't saying it then but looking back – there was very little way of getting back to them. I think the Final has always been remembered, in a way, because we were the so-called Quality Street Gang, with some big signings, and they were this hard-bitten hewn out of the rock team from a little Yorkshire town, all amateur rugby league lads who'd made it and come through. The Castleford lads had grown up together. You couldn't go a lot further than Hepworth and Hardisty as half-backs, and they had a supreme pack around at that time. I know the press said so, but I don't remember Wembley particularly as a dirty game, not at all. Rugby league is a very tough game. If you can't stand the heat don't go on the field!

Brian Snape turned defeat into celebration, having invited the whole Salford contingent – first team and reserve players, officials, wives and partners – to a post-match banquet at the Royal Garden Hotel in Kensington. As everybody dined, drank and danced to the sound of The Caribbeans – a steel band that also entertained at Salford's club – the despondency of a few hours earlier was lifted. 'I think that was down to Brian Snape' says Chris, 'I think he was so delighted to have reached the Final and it was a very close run game. The achievement for him was getting to Wembley and he insisted it was going to be a special night. We'd have liked the trophy there as well but it wasn't to be.'

The team returned by train to Piccadilly Station in Manchester to be met by an open top bus which took them to the Salford Art Gallery, on the Crescent, where they appeared on the balcony to be greeted by the fans. 'It was wonderful. Thousands and thousands of people turned out along the route. That was early days in my career with Salford and really we should have gone on to better things Wembley-wise but there's only two teams can go. But it was a great occasion and it was wonderful for Salford to get to the final. We were all very sad that we didn't win it for the supporters, who followed us everywhere, but it was a great weekend for them. It put a lot of pride back in Salford.'

5

LIVING THE
IMPOSSIBLE DREAM

Ever since he travelled on the team coach as a young player at Wigan listening to Eric Ashton and other senior players expounding on their experience of touring Australia and New Zealand, Chris had dreamt of one day emulating them. He probably thought it the impossible dream until, in March 1970, his name appeared amongst the list of players to depart on that year's tour just two months later. 'Being picked for the first time was great because I'd always wanted to tour,' says Chris, 'I wanted to play for Great Britain and I wanted to go to Australia and New Zealand. To be honest, it still came as a shock that it happened, because although people were bandying my name about as a candidate, it was the days of Frank Myler, Syd Hynes, John Atkinson and Alan Smith – all of them great three-quarters.'

Whilst his international career was making rapid strides, progress was also happening at club level. In 1969/70, Salford put their Wembley woes to the back of their mind, winning 22 of their 34 League fixtures – the best return at the club for 20 years – to maintain the sixth position they attained the previous season. Chris made the most appearances for the Red Devils, missing just one of the club's overall total of 42 games, and that due to international duty.

Despite the improvement in League results that season, there were no trophies won and no finals reached, a situation that would influence the dismissal of coach Griff Jenkins as the term drew to a close. During the opening months of the campaign, the team's form was indifferent, a massive disappointment for most, who expected them to be buoyed up from the achievement of reaching Wembley. Despite the ups and downs Chris was consistently singled out for praise by the rugby league press, his form maintaining a high standard throughout.

The opening fixture of 1969/70 was a visit to Huyton – formerly known as Liverpool City – on Sunday 10 August to mark the official opening of their new ground at Alt Park. Chris grabbed two of the Reds' 14 tries as the visitors spoilt the house-warming party with an emphatic 60-5 victory. The following weekend, however, the Reds' supporters witnessed the other extreme of their early season form with an inept display at Central Park. Despite the *Manchester Evening News* headline, which claimed 'Hesketh Is A Big Star For Salford', Wigan won comfortably enough by 25-9 in what was the opening round of the Lancashire Cup. Their rugby league correspondent Jack McNamara gave the Reds fans some crumbs of comfort, writing 'If Salford had a star, it was centre Chris Hesketh. He is a man who never admits defeat and without him Salford would have collapsed. Afterwards (Wigan captain Doug) Laughton, sweat streaming off his face, said "I don't know where Hesketh finds the energy. He never let up and had a rest like most of us."'

His excellent form kept Chris at the forefront with the county and international selectors. He appeared in both of Lancashire's fixtures during September – victories over Yorkshire at The Willows, and Cumberland at Derwent Park, securing the county championship – and represented England twice during October, Wales being beaten at Headingley, and France forcing a draw at Central Park. The latter was described as 'another French farce' due to the refereeing of Georges Jameau, because the French official, apparently, awarded two tries to his fellow countrymen after 'blatant' knock-ons. As with his club form, Chris rose above the turmoil, one hack noting that 'On the bright side, Salford's centre Hesketh gave a display on his native Wigan heath that fairly bristled with enthusiasm. Hesketh made the first and third English tries. He was undoubtedly the man of the match – with respect to the referee!'

Chris says 'I remember that match against France because Griff Jenkins came into the dressing room afterwards and said to me "You've had a good game. You're more or less on the plane now for the 1970 tour." I was thinking to myself "I hope I am, but it's not been picked yet mate!"' Nonetheless, despite his own reservations, Chris's reputation was growing rapidly. His no-nonsense, totally committed approach to every match endeared him to Salford's growing crowds, his unorthodox running style inspiring equally unorthodox nicknames such as the 'The Wriggler' and 'Merry-Legs.'

Colin Dixon used to call me 'snake hips' when we were playing 'tick and pass' at training, but I did it all without thinking. People would say 'How do you sidestep like that Chris?' And I'd say 'I don't know.' I'd see a situation in my mind and I'd go for it, whether it meant going outside or inside or up the middle or whatever. I probably didn't score a bagful of tries – although I still managed 128 for Salford, which isn't bad – but I'm a Wigan lad and I was brought up with the idea that centres were there to make tries for wingers. In my head was 'Get the winger in' because he can run faster than me and he'll probably score. I remember, when I played centre to Billy Boston in one match, he said 'Chris, what are you doing?' I said 'I'm trying to beat their centre and pull your winger away from you, then give you the ball.' He said 'Just give me the so-and-so ball, I'll do the rest!' So, I was giving him the ball while his own man was still marking him, but he could just whack him out of the way!

I didn't really learn off anybody because I was, without realising it, an individual as far as my running style went. I probably went the wrong way too many times as well, but I seemed to get away with it! I wouldn't survive with the so-called game plans of today because modern Super League coaches would say 'You've got to run down that part of the field' and I'd be somewhere else!

During October, Brian Snape dug deep into the Salford purse once again to produce two signings that created the press frenzy associated with David Watkins' arrival two years earlier and the Burgess–Dixon double spree that followed. Cardiff rugby union winger Maurice Richards – who the previous April had scored a record-equalling four tries for Wales against England at Twickenham – was signed, Cumbrian full-back Paul Charlton joining him two weeks later from Workington Town for a new rugby league record transfer fee of £12,500. Richards, who was to spend 14 years at The Willows, went on to make the most appearances recorded for the Reds, a total of 496 plus two more as a substitute, and claim the most tries for the club with an aggregate 297. Of the 385 starts that Chris was to make in the centre for Salford, 236 of those were with Richards as his left-wing partner. Charlton had been targeted by Salford for a while, having to upgrade their initial £5,000 offer several times before Town reluctantly parted with their prized asset. Whilst Charlton was already greatly admired by Chris, having played against him several times in county fixtures, Richards was destined to earn similar respect from his new three-quarter colleague:

Maurice was a real top class winger and one of the other things that made him a bit more special was he was a very hard man. He thought nothing of coming in off the wing and clouting the centre, and when I say 'clouting' I mean, of course, tackling! In actual fact, I wouldn't say he was electric paced but he was still quick, and he was strong. I could give him the ball going for the corner, and seven times out of 10, he'd be getting there and scoring. Maurice was a very nice guy, a quiet, private individual, not like me, always chatting and 'gobby.' He didn't really tell you much about his private life and we didn't ask. I haven't seen Maurice since the last pass I gave him. He did very well for Salford.

When Brian Snape came up to me and said 'How well do you know Paul Charlton?' I replied 'Now you're talking my language!' To me, he's the best full-back that ever played in my time, for all sorts of reasons, and he was brilliant at coming into the line and, of course, he broke the world try scoring record with 33 in 1972/73. We used to practice endlessly, Paul and myself, with him coming up by my shoulder to take a pass. We used to see how close we could get without actually treading on each other's feet or knocking each other over! He was probably one of the fastest full-backs I've ever seen and you couldn't fault his defence. He'd show anybody the corner and I don't think I've ever seen a winger go past him on the outside. We were playing once against Leigh at Hilton Park and Rodney Tickle – a real flyer – got away and Paul was shepherding him towards the corner. We were desperately trying to get across but Paul just put him over the touchline. The other thing about him was he absolutely loved his rugby and he was a fanatic trainer and tremendously fit. Paul and myself would always do a bit extra at training, just a few more sprints or whatever. I got on very well with him.

Both the new arrivals made their debuts in Wednesday evening fixtures at The Willows. Richards' bow, versus Leigh on 15 October, drew 11,606 spectators, whilst Charlton's – coupled with that of experienced 31-year-old prop Ken Roberts, acquired from Rochdale Hornets for £1,250 – two weeks later, against St Helens, brought in 11,300. The Reds won both matches, Chris stealing the limelight in the latter as he recorded two tries in the 16-12 verdict over the Saints.

One headline proclaimed 'Luck With Salford As Chris Outstars New Men', the match report saying that 'Chris Hesketh, the Wigan-born centre who starred for England in the sketchy international against France, was Salford's saviour last night. Switching to out-half in the absence of the injured David Watkins, Hesketh responded magnificently to play one of his most valuable games for the club – on the night Salford introduced Paul Charlton and Ken Roberts. Both had been signed in a £13,750 double deal less than 24 hours before. But it was Hesketh who stole the show, and finished player of the match. First he tiptoed 35 yards to get Salford's opening try after St Helens had gone ahead with two penalty goals. Then Hesketh jerked Salford back into the game midway through the second half when the score was 9-9 and the St Helens forwards were threatening a victory push. This time Hesketh – always up in support of the man with the ball – followed Ken Roberts almost to the Saints' posts. When the former Rochdale man found his way blocked, Hesketh took his pass to score his second try.'

A month later, Friday 28 November, Chris again made the headlines, the *Manchester Evening News* exclaiming 'Hesketh The Match Winner' for his part in the 17-12 success over Wakefield Trinity at The Willows. Trinity had led 7-2 at the halfway stage and looked like claiming the two League points on offer until Chris went over for the first of Salford's three second half tries, sidestepping his way past four defenders for a superb try which turned the course of the match.

At the beginning of March, he was rewarded for his endeavour, being one of 21 players selected for the 1970 tour party. A further five names were added three weeks later to complete the 26-man squad, when it was also announced that St Helens' Frank Myler would be captain. 'Frank is now a good friend of mine,' says Chris 'a brilliant bloke and as ordinary as you like. And, of course, he was to become the last Great Britain tour captain to win the Ashes. You can't do a lot better than that in rugby league can you?'

Chris shared with prop forward Johnny Ward the distinction of being the first Salford tourist since Irish-born hooker Tom McKinney made the trip in 1954. Ward had only joined the Reds the previous January, transferring for £6,000 from Castleford, where he had been a member of the team that conquered Salford at Wembley in 1969. Despite the loss of Ward, the Yorkshire side still contributed five of the tourists, as did Leeds:

What probably got Brian Snape to bring Johnny Ward to Salford was that he would roll in with the ball at Castleford. Two men would come in and tackle him and he'd have half-backs Keith Hepworth on one side and Alan Hardisty on the other and they made some good things happen from that. Johnny was magic with that ball. He was what I would call a 'rumbling' type of player, similar to Brian McTigue at Wigan, you know; 'Follow me and you'll get that pass', but at Salford we didn't play that sort of rugby in our forwards. We didn't drive in three, four or five times because we'd get beaten. We'd have second-row forwards like Colin Dixon or Mike Coulman on the outside of the line running at centres. That's why at the time we missed out so often at Salford, through not having a big strong up-the-middle pack, but we entertained and we enjoyed it. It was a different way of playing the game.

Watched by friends and relatives, who had made tearful farewells, the Great Britain party left Manchester Airport for a 36-hour flight, landing at Darwin Airport in Australia's Northern Territory late Thursday night, on 21 May. Facing them was a tough opening schedule of five matches in nine days, followed by the first Test, which was to be played in Brisbane. The opening few weeks of the tour was a bitter-sweet experience for Chris. It began well enough, appearing in the opening match against a Northern

Territory representative side at Darwin, just 18 hours after embarking from an arduous flight. Chris scored two of the tries, including the first of the tour on the way to a convincing 35-12 victory:

> I can still remember that first try. I got on the outside of a move and I just finished it off. All I had to do was run it in, but in my mind, I was saying 'Just imagine – the first try of the tour!' It was an 8 o'clock kick-off at night because it was very hot, and I remember that an iguana came onto the field! The lads and myself were saying 'What the hell's that thing?' because we'd never seen anything like it before. Somebody just ran on and chased it off. It was quite a big beast and, at that time I didn't even know what an iguana was.

His upbeat mood was dented during his second appearance, against Central Queensland at Rockhampton, the third match of the tour. 'I got tackled upstairs and my leg was down and another fellah came in and stood on my ankle' recalls Chris, 'and I knew straight away it was bad. The studs went to the bone and it really hurt. They took me to hospital where I had to have stitches put in it.' His initial fear was that he would have to return home, but, following nearly two weeks' convalescence and light training, he resumed his place on the field. Midway through his period of inactivity, however, Chris's injury woes paled into insignificance when he received news from England that he had dreaded:

> I was in our hotel in Brisbane and somebody knocked on my room door and woke me in the night. It was a telegram from my brother Gerard, saying our dad had passed away. He was very ill before I left home and I'm sure he knew he was dying but he never said anything. He'd been ill for a long time with cancer. I had mixed feelings about the tour, but my dad would have said 'Go' because he knew that was everything to

me and it was to him, obviously. It's something you strive for all your playing career but I'd hoped he'd live at least until I got back. It was impossible to get home for the funeral and it must have been an awful time for my mam and my brothers and sister. Obviously, it did take the edge off the tour for me but I had to get on with it. I'm sure my dad would have wanted me to. He was still comparatively young and, even now, I wish he was still alive.

Doing his best to put his terrible loss to the back of his mind, Chris reappeared for the tourists in the match against Toowoomba, played on Sunday, 7 June. It took place the day after Britain lost the opening Test against Australia 37-15, subsequently turning the series around by winning the remaining Tests, the last time, to date, Britain claimed an Ashes series. On Tuesday 23 June, Chris played for the tourists against the Sydney Colts at Endeavour Field, promoted as the 'Captain Cook Commemorative Match', in honour of Cook's discovery of Australia 200 years earlier, having sailed around the world in his ship, 'Endeavour.' The match was organised by the Cronulla-Sutherland Leagues' Club and the tourists each received a magnificent bi-centenary medal, which Chris still has.

His chance to shine at Test level arrived when he was picked for the third in the series against New Zealand – the penultimate match of the tour – on Saturday 25 July at Carlaw Park, Auckland. With the centre berths firmly tied up by the experienced duo of Hynes and Myler, and Roger Millward occupying the stand-off position, Chris had been unable to claim a Test spot thus far on the tour, although, to be fair, he had not really expected to do so. In what was his first ever Test appearance, he contributed a try towards the resounding 33-16 win over the Kiwis, helping to complete a 3-0 whitewash. The Great Britain line-up was: Dutton (Widnes), Smith (Leeds), Hesketh (Salford), Myler (St Helens), Atkinson (Leeds), Millward (Hull Kingston Rovers), Hepworth

(Castleford), Watson (St Helens), Fisher (Bradford Northern), Ward (Salford), Irving (Oldham), Lowe (Hull Kingston Rovers), Reilly (Castleford). Substitutes: Hynes (Leeds), Laughton (Wigan). Despite his sorrow at losing his father, Chris returned home with some happy tour memories, particularly of his comrades:

Ray Dutton and myself roomed together all through the tour. Ray was always a very good friend of mine, and a very amusing man. He was always singing a Tom Jones song, or something like that, and, of course, he was a good full-back and all. A few days before the final Test in New Zealand, we played West Coast at Greymouth. I remember it was awful weather. Only the team that was playing travelled from our base, and we went on this single-line train that was really old fashioned. When we got to Greymouth, we stayed overnight in a wooden hotel and Ray and myself went out walking. You do a lot of that on tour, going out for a walk. People say 'You're always in night clubs on tour' but I can honestly say 'No, we weren't.'

Peter 'Flash' Flanagan, the Hull Kingston Rovers hooker, was a great character on that tour, if ever there was one. He was also a funny man to be with and another who liked to impersonate people. He was a good player, very industrious and constantly coming in as acting half-back. Bobby Irving, who had to postpone his wedding to go on the tour, was a very powerful lad to have around and he scored a lot of tries for a second row forward. Doug Laughton was a cracking loose forward and Roger Millward was another wonderful player to have around and a wonderful man to be with. He was absolutely brilliant.

Great Britain lost just one match – the opening Test to Australia – during their 24-match schedule, Chris appearing 13 times – nine in Australia and four in New Zealand – and scoring nine tries. The success of the trip was due, in part, to good leadership from tour manager, the Leigh chairman Jack Harding, and assistant tour manager and coach, Johnny Whiteley of Hull. 'I still see Johnny occasionally' says Chris. 'He always kept himself fit and, consequently, he still looks very fit now. Johnny hardly slept on tour. He was one of those people who would always be available to give a rub down or provide a bandage or whatever 24 hours of the day. Obviously, he did sleep, but it seemed like he never did. He was a dream coach and he had a damn good team. There was a good mixture of players who were just about right at the time to beat the Aussies.' There is no doubt the know-how Chris gained on the 1970 tour stood him in good stead for the even greater honour bestowed on him by the selectors four years later.

6

ON TOP OF THE WORLD

Chris arrived back from the 1970 tour battered and bruised, and ready for a rest rather than having to dive headfirst into the rigours of the domestic 1970/71 season, a schedule referred to today as 'back-to-back' rugby. Chris says 'I remember getting back and Brian Snape was waiting for me at Manchester Airport. He said to me "Have you had a good tour? Will you play in the St Helens Sevens this weekend?" I thought to myself "Bloody Hell!"' Never one to say 'No', Chris obliged, helping his team win 'The Saints Sevens Trophy' beating the hosts 28-16 in the final, just seven days after taking part in the third Test against New Zealand in Auckland. Snape, though, was a generous soul who appreciated the need to look after his players and, afterwards, despatched Chris and family to Blackpool to enjoy a welcome break at the Stuart Hotel.

Chris returned to action at Keighley in a pre-season friendly on 14 August, commencing a personal run of 16 consecutive appearances for Salford. Two weeks later a headline read 'Hesketh Has 'Em In A Spin' after Salford had played brilliantly at Watersheddings in defeating Oldham 35-12 in the first round of the Lancashire Cup. The writer said 'Speedy Salford centre Chris Hesketh baffled lowly Oldham. His elusive sidesteps, body-swerves and dummies split the Oldham cover wide apart. And it was the nippy Hesketh who made the openings for nearly all of his side's seven tries, grabbing two himself.'

He came to the fore again when Salford achieved an emphatic

36-6 win at Castleford on 16 September, ending a sequence of nine defeats – including Wembley – at the hands of their Yorkshire rivals. Chris weighed in with two tries, one report stating 'Chris Hesketh's straight running often had Castleford in trouble, and his 40-yard burst for Salford's second try illustrated more than anything the sharp difference in pace between the back divisions.'

It was early October when Chris vacated his place in Salford's team, albeit temporarily and for the best of reasons. Having made his mark 'Down Under' in a Great Britain jersey, he was included in their 19-man squad to compete in the 1970 World Cup, held in England. Coming so soon after the tour, the competition was a big 'Ask' for the 15 players selected who had returned home just two months earlier. One of the four new names was Chris's Salford colleague Paul Charlton, making up for his surprise omission from the tour. There was continuity with Jack Harding and Johnny Whiteley being in charge once more and Frank Myler retaining the captaincy.

Chris was one of the two substitutes for the opening games against Australia, at Headingley on Saturday 24 October, and France, at Castleford four days later. Both were won although Chris did not get a taste of the action in either. He was, however, given a starting role at centre for the next match. Deputising for an injured Myler, he scored a try in the convincing 27-17 win over New Zealand at Swinton on 31 October.

The World Cup Final was at Headingley on Saturday 7 November, Great Britain facing Australia with the knowledge that they had already defeated their Colonial cousins 11-4 in the group stage. The Final was a niggling, bad tempered affair, which resulted in Australia's Billy Smith and Britain's Syd Hynes being dismissed by Wakefield whistler Fred Lindop in the second half, followed by further on-field skirmishes after the match ended. Australia won 12-7 but Chris, at least, had the satisfaction of facing them for the first time at international level when he was brought on as a replacement for Myler. The Great Britain team for the

Final was: Dutton (Widnes), Smith (Leeds), Hynes (Leeds), Myler (St Helens), Atkinson (Leeds), Shoebottom (Leeds), Hepworth (Castleford), Hartley (Castleford), Fisher (Leeds), Watson (St Helens), Thompson (Featherstone Rovers), Laughton (Wigan), Reilly (Castleford). Substitutes: Hesketh (Salford), Haigh (Leeds).

His first World Cup adventure over, Chris rejoined his Salford colleagues at The Willows. One crucial difference that season was that former Swinton and St Helens coach Cliff Evans had replaced the departed Griff Jenkins, an appointment confirmed in May shortly after Chris had left with the tourists. Evans was a former rugby union half-back from Wales who had turned professional with Salford in the 1930s and later went on to play with distinction for Leeds. His first season back at The Willows coincided with the emergence of two talented halves who – as a pair – would serve the club well over the next five seasons. Stand-off Ken Gill was signed from St Helens amateur club, Pilkington Recs, in September 1970, scrum-half Peter Banner from Spotland Rangers, based in Rochdale, during 1967. They rose like a Phoenix during the latter half of the 1970/71 campaign, following stunning performances in the reserves, to establish themselves as first choice pairing. In the process, they replaced David Watkins and Bob Prosser, the regular choice up to that point, Evans taking the brave, but adventurous decision to relocate Watkins to the centre, a move that was to pay dividends for both Salford and the charismatic Welshman:

> Cliff Evans was subtlety gone mad, he was a real tactician. Unlike modern rugby league players I never really played to a game plan in my life. The closest I came to it was under Cliff Evans. After Cliff arrived we had certain moves. We'd just shout a name. 'Torquay' was one of them, and there was another called 'Double Double'. There was one that we called 'Billy In', which came from Wigan. It was a move developed to bring Billy Boston in off the touchline at a scrum inside the opponents' 25. At the end of the move, you

would just pop it up for him and he was next door to being unstoppable in that situation. We didn't have a Billy Boston at Salford but we still called it 'Billy In.' We used to use Mike Coulman for that sometimes. Mike was big, strong, and fast, and I wouldn't like to have stopped him! Cliff exploited the guile of Kenny Gill in the middle and the power offered by Paul Charlton, when he burst into our line. I suppose we did have a game plan then but we weren't telling anybody!

Cliff was a good coach and a brilliant man but you've got to remember as well, though, that he had the tools – in terms of players – at the time. Kenny Gill being available to him was a big item because Kenny was a very, very good stand-off who was discovered by Albert White, Salford's chief scout and a director, and, when you think, there were loads of clubs around St Helens who didn't pick him up. I had a lot of time for Kenny. He could run but he was short of a yard of pace and he didn't take people on very often, but his brain was doing something else. If he ever went through a gap it was more or less a dummy move. Whoever you were playing against they'd say 'Keep an eye on him trying to set up this and that.' He wasn't the same as other half-backs. He had a unique style and his pass into a gap or space was weighted to perfection. And he was a brave lad as well. He got knocked about and received a few late tackles. I've got to say I played very well with Kenny Gill around.

Peter Banner was a very useful scrum-half, mainly because of his pace and also because he ran close to the ground and he was difficult to defend against. He didn't run stood up, he just ducked and weaved but he was a wonderful half-back. David Watkins put a massive injection of pace and many other things into Salford, and he brought the crowds in, but David was a rugby union stand-off and rugby union stand-offs very rarely get tackled – or then they didn't anyway. His move to the centre worked very well.

Rochdale Hornets travelled to The Willows towards the end of March and, although losing 18-9, they had clearly done their homework on the Reds' new half-back pairing. In a bad tempered affair, during which Salford's Charlie Bott and Rochdale's Mike Watson were given marching orders, Jack McNamara observed in the *Manchester Evening News* that 'Hornets marked Peter Banner and Ken Gill, Salford's dashing young halves, so closely that they were rarely allowed to produce any tricks, and it was left to centre Chris Hesketh to stir the crowd with a wonderful 50-yard solo try.'

With the 1970/71 season drawing to a conclusion and vital League points needed to claim a good position in the final table ahead of the play-offs, Salford visited their great rivals Swinton for the traditional Easter holiday meeting on Saturday 10 April. In what was an entertaining and exciting derby match – despite the dismissals of Bill Kirkbride (Salford) and Kevin Whittle (Swinton) – the Red Devils were trailing 20-18 with seconds remaining. As Chris was attempting to play the ball on the edge of the Swinton 25-yard area, the referee judged that he had been fouled, awarding a penalty. Salford's Paul Jackson placed the ball down from what looked a kickable position in the hope of forcing a draw. Thus, the stage was set for Chris to produce one of his most memorable moments. Throughout his career, he had persevered with the habit of following up every penalty kick attempt and this time it produced dividends. Jackson's kick hit the upright and bounced out, dropping beneath the posts. Chris was first on the scene and amongst a melee of defenders managed to get the touchdown, Jackson's conversion cementing a 23-20 triumph:

I said to Paul 'Try and hit the upright' and he did. I was joking of course! I just wanted him to kick the goal. It came straight down and they were all trying to get to the ball but I just went in and scored. I've followed up thousands of kicks. This time it paid off. To me, it's 'track-suit' coaching or leadership. If I'm doing it every time then I'm basically leading from the front. It rarely happened, when it hit the post and came back, but on many other occasions the ball was fumbled by a defender or, if someone was trying to run it out, I tackled him near their line. When I was playing for West Park Grammar School, I remember when I followed the ball after a penalty and it landed on the cross-bar, came out and fell into my arms. Although I didn't score on that occasion I think that's when it all started.

It was also at the business end of the season that stories surfaced in the press implying Chris was planning a return to the Antipodes to appear in club rugby. During February one back page headline informed us 'Hesketh May Get Kiwi Job', the writer of the piece claiming the 26-year-old Wiganer had been offered a house, a car and a job to become a player–coach at Wellington in New Zealand. According to reports, club colleague Watkins had turned down a similar approach, and attention was now focused on Chris. The following month, another report said 'Chris Hesketh has been refused permission by his club to accept an offer to coach New Zealand club Wellington this summer' all of which Chris finds difficult to fathom today. 'I remember it coming out in the papers but I never spoke to anybody from Wellington, which puts it to bed really' he says. 'At the time people said to me "Are you going to New Zealand?" and I replied "No." As far as the club refusing permission goes I didn't even know about it.'

A month later – April 1971 – another revelation appeared in the press claiming glamorous Australian club St George were chasing his signature. A report said 'Chris Hesketh is the latest Great Britain player to be chased by wealthy Australian clubs. Sydney St George, on the lookout for world-class backs, have wanted him since he starred on tour "Down Under" last summer. Now they are prepared to offer him a contract worth £3,000 a year if he decides to emigrate.' In this instance, Chris acknowledges the story is correct:

There was a bloke whose name was Bill Summerell who was connected with St George. He did talk to me quite a lot of times during the 1970 tour and wrote to me for several years afterwards. Brian Snape had a word or two with me about it when I came off the tour and it was all very amicable. I remember he said to me 'Chris, if you went we'd have to spend x amount of money to replace you.' I suppose going to Sydney St George would have been the one to choose wouldn't it? They won 11 championships on the trot from 1956 to 1966. I was flattered by their interest but, you've got to realise, I'd only just lost my dad and it was a difficult enough time for my mam without me leaving.

Salford finished the 1970/71 League campaign in seventh place, a drop of one position from the previous year. It earned a home tie in the opening round of the top-16 play-off on 25 April, when Chris and his colleagues comfortably disposed of Halifax by 33-3. Their reward was a visit to Leeds in the next stage on 1 May. In a 13-try bonanza described as 'a scoring spree in the sunshine' Salford lost 37-22 but the repercussion from the match extended beyond merely being eliminated from the Championship.

The following day, in his *Sunday Mirror* match report, Eddie Waring wrote 'Mick Shoebottom could face a grim struggle to be fit for the Rugby League Challenge Cup Final at Wembley a week on Saturday. The Leeds half-back star was kept in hospital last night after being accidentally kicked by Salford forward Colin Dixon, and he may have a fractured jaw.' The incident, which occurred as Shoebottom dived over the line for one of the Leeds tries, resulted in the player suffering from 'severe concussion' as well as receiving what was confirmed as a broken jaw.

Close on six months later, on 30 October 1971, the Reds were back at Headingley to take on Leeds in a League fixture. By this time, Shoebottom's health had deteriorated and, not only did he miss that 1971 Wembley date, but, sadly, he never played for

Leeds again. Dixon was targeted throughout the afternoon by the opposition, both players and spectators. One Salford player was quoted as saying 'Leeds had it in for Dixon from the start and gave him a hammering', another commenting 'The behaviour of some spectators was just childish. I've never seen anything like it.' The Salford team required police protection after the match as supporters invaded the pitch with Chris, reportedly, being amongst those punched by spectators as they tried to return to the dressing room:

> Colin Dixon was not a dirty player. I never saw Colin knowingly – and I can only speak as I find – going out to damage somebody. In my mind's eye I can see Shoey going down in that corner to score and Dicko going over with him and tackling him. Whatever way he tackled Shoey I don't recall after all this time but there's no way he went looking to damage him to that extent. I think it's pretty awful that people still bring it up in that way now. I remember when we went back to Leeds the crowd was around our team coach as we left, shouting and jeering.

In his summation to the 1970/71 season, Tom Bergin had written in the *Salford City Reporter* that 'After a not surprising staleness after his tasks on tour in Australia and in the World Cup, Chris Hesketh emerged as one of the giants of the team'. There was no such distraction for the start of the following term, the 1971 close season affording Chris the luxury of his first break from rugby in almost two years. Recharged and refreshed, he was off to a much quicker start for 1971/72, producing sparkling form as soon as the curtain went up, helping the Reds win their first eight Championship matches, the club's best opening to a League campaign since 1933/34.

Having appeared for Great Britain in both Tests against France earlier in the year at the Stade Municipal, Toulouse (in February), and Knowsley Road, St Helens (March), Chris's eye-catching displays ensured he retained his place for the opening Test against the 1971 New Zealand tourists. Staged at The Willows on 25 September, Chris managed to claim one of Britain's three tries on his home turf but it was insufficient to stop the Kiwis winning 18-13. Four days later he savoured one of his proudest moments when leading Lancashire out of the tunnel at Leigh for the Roses clash with Yorkshire. It was the first time in his professional career he had been selected as a team captain, although losing on that occasion 42-22.

Chris retained his place in Britain's side for the remaining two Tests, but it was a disappointing outcome for home fans, New Zealand clinching the series through a 17-14 win at Castleford on 16 October, their hosts saving face at Headingley on 6 November with a 12-3 verdict in their favour. In a 1974 interview Chris confessed to Brian Batty of the *Daily Mail* that "This was a disappointing series against New Zealand, because we lost after having quite a lot of bad luck with injuries, even though the tour side turned on some fine football.'

There is, at least, one fond memory for Chris from the Kiwis visit in 1971. On Friday 22 October a powerful looking New Zealand line-up containing ten Test regulars took on Salford under The Willows floodlights. Salford won 31-30, McNamara saying, incredulously, 'Despite having slept on it, the whole match still seems slightly unreal.' Chris, who began the game in the centre but moved to stand-off after scrum-half Peter Banner retired with injury, says 'It particularly stands in my memory because of the unusual score and the change round in fortunes over the 80 minutes. We were running all over them in the first half and they were getting hammered. By half-time it was 26-0 but they came back strongly and we only just won.'

Chris's luck deserted him in the 25-9 home win over Castleford on 10 December when he sustained an injury to his left knee that required a cartilage operation. On this occasion, it kept him away from the action until early March, but it was an injury that plagued him throughout the rest of his career. Apart from taking him out of contention for Great Britain's two Tests with France in the opening months of 1972, his ten-match absence from the Salford side cost him his place in the first round home Challenge Cup tie with Wigan. Salford had had high hopes of a Wembley return following two quarter-final exits away to bogey club Castleford in 1970 and 1971. The unavailability of Chris and play-maker Ken Gill – out with a broken jaw – did not help their cause, Salford's ambition being dashed once more with a 16-12 defeat in front of 17,900.

Having recovered, he took part in the final 12 matches of the season and quickly recaptured his earlier zest, helping his team-mates to a fifth place finish in the League table, the highest for 25 years. Salford gained some consolation for the Challenge Cup defeat with a 21-9 win over Wigan at Central Park in the second round of the Championship play-off before again going down to Leeds at Headingley in the semi-final, the eventual Champions winning 10-0. McNamara commented 'Only centre Chris Hesketh gave Leeds much worry on attack. There was a hint of desperation about Hesketh's efforts to crack the defence. He made several solo runs from the play-the-ball and chased every kick as if the ball were gold. Nobody else made such a nuisance of himself to Leeds. Hesketh played like an extra forward, a role he had to fill when prop Terry Ramshaw went off in the second half with an ankle injury.'

Salford did not make their customary end-of-season return to Headingley for the Leeds Sevens. The Reds had won the competition three years running in 1968, 1969 and 1970, suffering a surprise first round defeat to St Helens in 1971. Snape, upset over the Dixon incident, said at that time Salford would not be entering the competition again. In the event, tempers cooled and it was announced to the press they were standing down for the 1972 contest only, citing 'team problems' adding 'David Watkins has knee trouble and the joint is in plaster.' Salford did take part again in 1974, winning for a fourth time, although Chris – along with Watkins – did not share that success through tour commitments.

Early into the 1972/73 season – during September – Snape broke the rugby league transfer record for a third time with the £13,500 capture of St Helens back-row forward Eric Prescott. 'Eric was a very quick, hard working forward and covered a lot of ground' recalls Chris, 'He wasn't what you'd call a big forward although, at the same time, he was a big winger, which is where he started out at St Helens. Eric scored a lot of tries for Salford and his tackling rate was pretty good too.'

Whilst Chris had patiently waited five years for his first winners' medal with Salford, Prescott managed to achieve that objective in as many weeks. Salford were on £60 a man and 25 pence a point for the 1972 Lancashire Cup semi-final meeting with Wigan at Central Park on 6 October, so determined were club officials to bring success to the club. Whether or not the financial incentive did the trick, the Reds reached the Final on the back of an emphatic 14-2 win. McNamara wrote: 'Two high spots of an entertaining match were Chris Hesketh's try after a neat scrum move starring stand-off Ken Gill that could not have been programmed better by computer, and a thrilling solo run by Paul Charlton.'

Salford warmed up for their Final date against Swinton by securing a double over Blackpool Borough. The Reds defeated the Fylde coast outfit 37-10 on their visit to the seaside, just two days after their triumph at Wigan, and 43-13 at The Willows on 13 October when 'The best try came from centre Chris Hesketh after a delightful double scissors with scrum-half Peter Banner.'

A week later, on 21 October, Salford and Swinton squared up to each other in the Lancashire Cup Final at Warrington. Salford paraded the following line-up: Charlton, Eastham, Watkins, Hesketh, Richards, Gill, Banner, MacKay, Walker, Ward, Whitehead, Dixon, Prescott. Subs: Orr, Davies.

It was Chris, in the 24th minute, who initiated the move leading to the first of Salford's five tries. One report said 'Chris Hesketh broke clear with a smart change of pace, Colin Dixon took over and threw a long pass which Ken Gill took with a juggling act. He then pushed the ball along for Maurice Richards to touch down.' It gave Salford a slender 3-2 lead, extended to a 10-4 advantage by half-time when Watkins went over for a second try just before the break. Swinton threatened to take control at the start of the second period but, with the score standing at 10-6 following a Swinton drop-goal from the boot of Peter Kenny, Chris rose to the challenge once more when he broke away again in the 51st minute. Bergin described it thus: 'Hesketh beat man after man in a splendid attack down the middle and when he sucked in the two remaining opponents there was Charlton to take the ball and run 50 yards for an unforgettable try at the corner.'

His initiative gave the Red Devils valuable breathing space although the 'never-say-die' attitude of the Lions reduced the deficit to 13-11 through a fine try from winger Bob Fleay before Salford added the finishing touches with two late touchdowns from Phil Eastham and Banner. John Robinson of *The People* said that Chris, through his 'experience and know-how guided Salford when the going got tough', which was particularly true in the first half and the early stages of the second when the match was tightly fought and no quarter asked or given. Chris remembers 'It was my first medal, except for the A team one when I was at Wigan. To be fair, the final was won more by our forwards. I think that was probably because we were in our first big final for many a year and you had to play it tight until you got enough in front to be safe.' The 25-11 score-line brought the first major trophy to The Willows since 1939, the players being further rewarded by Snape through a £100-a-man pay packet and a holiday in Majorca.

There was precious little time to celebrate for three of the Salford players. At the beginning of October, Chris, plus colleagues Charlton and Dixon, had been told of their inclusion in

Great Britain's list of 19 players to travel to France for the 1972 World Cup, commencing the weekend after the county final. Curiously, although it had only been two years since the previous tournament, the only survivors in the British camp were Chris, Charlton and Leeds' John Atkinson.

Whilst the club was delighted to see their players gain international recognition, it created nervousness at The Willows when they were included in a Great Britain 'trial' side to face Oldham at Watersheddings just three days before the clash with Swinton. The club appealed, unsuccessfully, for them to be excused. Thankfully, no one was injured!

The 1972 World Cup firmly established Chris as a stand out player in the Great Britain set-up, particularly after his awesome display in the Final against Australia. *Open Rugby* editor, Harry Edgar, wrote of Chris in 1979: 'His first major impact on international rugby came in the 1972 World Cup in France. In one of Britain's finest hours, Hesketh's unflinching mid-field defence did so much to weaken the effect of Australia's fearsome Mark Harris in that tension filled final at Lyon.' Britain reached the Final after achieving a 100 per cent success rate from their three group matches:

The 27-21 victory over Australia, at the Stade Gilbert Brutus in Perpignan on Sunday 29 October, won us the World Cup really because they had it all to do after that. Then, three days later, at the Stade Municipal in Grenoble, which is a beautiful place, we beat France 13-4, and, finally, the following Saturday, we won quite easily against New Zealand 53-19. I scored a try in that match, but I particularly remember the performance of John Holmes the Leeds stand-off. He scored two tries and ten goals, which is not bad going in a World Cup game. It was played at Le Stade du Hameau in Pau, south-west France. Now that I'm no longer playing rugby I really would like to go back there because it's a wonderful city and I never really got the chance to look at it.

With a week to go before the World Cup Final on Saturday 11 November, the Great Britain squad flew back home on the previous Monday morning, reconvening for a training session at Headingley the following Thursday afternoon. The day afterwards, the players travelled in two coaches – some from Leeds, some from Manchester – to East Midlands Airport to catch a midday flight to Lyon, the Final being staged there at the Stade de Gerland. Chris was selected at right centre with skipper Clive Sullivan as his winger, the pair having occupied the right flank in the three previous games. The team was: Charlton (Salford), Sullivan (Hull), Hesketh (Salford), Walsh (St Helens), Atkinson (Leeds), Holmes (Leeds), Nash (Featherstone Rovers), Clawson (Leeds), Stephenson (Dewsbury), Jeanes (Leeds), Lowe (Hull Kingston Rovers), Lockwood (Castleford), Nicholls (Widnes). Substitutes: Irving (Oldham), D O'Neill (Widnes).

Chris was to play a significant role in Great Britain's crucial opening try just before half-time. The Australian's were already 5-2 up – their prop John O'Neill having scored a try in the corner – and pressing for further points just inside Britain's 25-yard area. As they moved the ball threateningly towards the left flank, Chris nullified the danger when he tackled prop Bob O'Reilly so ferociously that the Australian lost the ball as he attempted to pass to the supporting Graeme Langlands. Quick as a flash, Sullivan, in one of rugby league's most memorable moments, scooped up the ball before going on a thrilling 75-yard run, hugging the right touchline to outpace the Aussie defence and plant the ball firmly in the corner. Agonisingly Terry Clawson's tricky goal attempt hit the top of the post and went wide, leaving the scores level at 5-5 when the half-time break came.

On the resumption, Australia regained the initiative to go 10-5 in front. It set up a tremendous barrage by the Aussies who sought to consolidate their advantage, Chris being particularly prominent at the heart of the British defence in holding them at bay. The tide turned with one of the best British moves of the final when Sullivan, with seven minutes left, played the role of inspirational captain once more. Spotting an opening, he cut inside, transferring the ball to Brian Lockwood, who bamboozled the defence before sending Mick Stephenson – later to gain fame as a Sky Television commentator – in for the try. Clawson's conversion made it 10-10. With rain now pouring down on the combatants, the final dramatically went into 20 minutes extra time, but there was no further score and Britain took the coveted trophy by virtue of their superior record in the group stage.

After a tightly fought contest Chris was given huge credit for the way he had snuffed out the danger posed by Australia's giant centre Mark Harris. There was one particularly jarring head-on collision when he stopped Harris dead in his tracks. After the match Chris was quoted as saying 'It hurt me but I think it hurt him as well. After that he always tried to cut through sideways. Actually I enjoyed tackling him.'

The final was a typical Great Britain-Australia game. The hardest games you can play are against the Aussies. They'd not picked me out to mark Mark Harris but he was a handful, a big lad and really strong and hard. He would have been very dangerous and I had to look after him. It was a long, hard match and you couldn't believe that it finished up as a draw. Just imagine having to go that extra 20 minutes and keep your nose just in front against Australia enough to win it. One slip and it was gone.

Its funny really because we won the World Cup, and you can see the photographs of us running round the stadium with the trophy, but then we came back home to East Midlands Airport, got the coach back to Manchester Victoria Station – the Yorkshire lads travelled back to Leeds – and we went straight home. There was nothing made of it. We didn't even get a medal. Bill Fallowfield, the Rugby Football League secretary at the time, eventually had little wooden plaques made and we all got one. But I now have a lovely World Cup winners' medal that I received at the British Lions Reunion at Pembroke Halls in Walkden in 1999. The 1954 and 1960 Great Britain World Cup winners were also presented with medals. I think they called our names out for the presentations and then took photographs of us all.

In reviewing the tournament, Geoff Prenter, editor of Australian sports paper *Rugby League Week*, included Chris in his World XIII, based on performances in the competition, saying 'Hesketh is the complete centre. He is tough, he is a thinker, he steps well, he tackles with extreme vigour.'

7

THAT CHAMPION FEELING

Following the heady heights of World Cup glory, Chris returned to the bread-and-butter world of domestic rugby league with Salford. At The Willows, players, officials and supporters were still basking in the glory of capturing the Lancashire Cup in the opening months of the 1972/73 season, and the Red Devils were hunting more silverware in the shape of the Players' No.6 Trophy, a knock-out contest that had been launched the previous season. Salford earned a semi-final date with Hull Kingston Rovers on 30 December. At the time, the competition – which was shelved after the last winter rugby league season of 1995/96 – did not cater for neutral venues at the penultimate stage. Consequently, the Reds faced the daunting task of meeting their rivals at the Rovers' Craven Park enclosure, having suffered a 17-14 first round exit there the previous term.

Salford arrived a day early, staying overnight in Hull to be fresher for the match. But it was the home side that looked livelier after the kick-off, over-running Salford with three unconverted tries in the opening 15 minutes. Somehow, they clung on and, with David Watkins landing three penalties, trailed only 9-6 at the interval. In a match televised live by the BBC, Salford came out looking the more determined set in the second half, scoring the only try through Maurice Richards and, with six minutes left, were level at 13-13. It was at that point that Colin Dixon dropped a goal to steal the match for the visitors. It was the first drop goal of his career and the only goal he ever scored for Salford!

In a competition where timetables had to conform to television schedules, the Final – against Leeds at Huddersfield – was almost three months off and the Salford players, meantime, focused their minds on other matters. On 28 January, with a 13-match winning streak behind them, they travelled to Featherstone carrying high hopes of winning their first round Rugby League Challenge Cup tie and pushing on towards Wembley. But, starved of possession from a scrum count of 19-4 against, Salford again crashed out, the Post Office Road side winning 18-11 on their way to lifting the coveted trophy at the Twin Towers. Having once more reserved one of their more inept performances for a cup match – as Salford tended to do during this period – they returned to their brilliant best for the following week's League fixture, easily overcoming Whitehaven 25-7 at The Willows. Chris scored the games outstanding try when racing over from halfway, his performance described as being as 'determined and competitive as ever.'

Chris was enjoying his best season to date, although Eric Shaw, writing in the *Rugby Leaguer*, reckoned that his dependable, consistent form, week in, week out, was not reflected by Salford supporters in their voting slips, handed in during the course of the season to determine the club's player of the year. He wrote: 'Consider the effort Hesketh puts in, that his winger is the leading try scorer, at least half of Paul Charlton's tries have come from running off Hesketh, and the devastating tackling that has blocked up the centre for Salford and Great Britain. Hesketh is steady rather than spectacular and this has cost him votes.'

On 9 March, Salford registered their eighteenth win in 19 matches – the cup exit at Featherstone being the spoiler – through defeating Dewsbury 15-7 at The Willows in a match described by the *Manchester Evening News* as 'flowing entertainment' with Chris pleasing the home fans, as always, with his 'virtuoso moments.' That result placed Salford joint top of the Championship table with Leeds, having both won 21 of their 26 League fixtures. In the next two matches, however, Salford's express train came temporarily off the rails. First up was a trip to St Helens on Friday evening, 16 March, the Reds being well beaten 21-4. Immediately afterwards, coach Cliff Evans, trainer Les Bettinson, and 22 players – including Chris – caught a midnight flight to Majorca, Brian Snape's promised reward for lifting the Lancashire Cup. Several writers suggested that the late flight to the sunshine occupied the players' minds more than St Helens had!

Having spent a weekend in Magaluf, the party returned home on Monday evening with the prospect of finally getting to grips with Leeds to contest ownership of the Players' No.6 Trophy. The Final, which saw Salford hit their second blip, was staged on Saturday 24 March at Fartown. Chris had created some concern in the Reds camp ahead of the match when it was reported he 'had to see a specialist about a septic ankle during Salford's weekend trip to Majorca. But after treatment he will be fit to play in Saturday's Players' No. 6 Trophy Final.'

Salford were on £134 a man to win the Final and, after only three minutes play, it looked as though they could be pocketing the cash, when Dixon went over for a try, which Watkins converted. Two great tries by Leeds winger John Atkinson, that put his team 10-5 ahead at half-time, turned the match. After the interval it developed into a dour forward battle, each side adding a penalty as Leeds claimed the day with a 12-7 win. Jack McNamara wrote of Salford in his *Manchester Evening News* match report that 'Peter Banner played bravely at scrum half and centres Chris Hesketh and David Watkins always looked capable of doing some damage without getting the chances to do so.' Once again, Salford's pack was seen to have fallen short on the big occasion, coach Evans saying 'We were forced into playing the sort of game we are not good at – crashing and bashing in the middle.'

I can remember the Final against Leeds, particularly because of the fact that we'd been away to Majorca the week before. After the St Helens night match we went straight to Manchester Airport and we landed at Palma at 4 o'clock in the morning, which was a bit daft, I suppose, being in the middle of the season. I don't honestly think the trip made any difference to our performance at St Helens or in the Final. But it was disappointing losing to Leeds in as much as we were always striving to get some silverware at Salford and, again, it resulted in another losers' medal.

Salford returned to the business of aiming for a good League position, but three defeats in the remaining seven games saw them slide down the table to finish sixth. One of the matches that they did win – 18-10 at home to Oldham on 13 April – saw Chris in stunning form; intercepting a pass after eight minutes for Maurice Richards to score and adding one himself later. It was a performance that earned Chris a new nickname, courtesy of *Manchester Evening News* writer Brian Bearshaw, who exclaimed 'Hesketh was magnificent. Whatever this man does, he does well and with the pride of a craftsman. He defended tirelessly, he attacked splendidly. He is so elusive he should have been cast as the Artful Dodger!'

Although his performance did not earn him a part in the musical hit 'Oliver!', it seemed that Chris had made an imprint on the minds of Oldham's officials. The headline 'Oldham Fancy Hesketh' appeared later that month when, according to the report, he was their ideal candidate as player–coach in succession to Wigan-bound Graham Starkey. Worryingly for Salford supporters, the story resurfaced a month later when Chris was quoted as saying 'It's up to Oldham to approach Salford. Obviously I'm interested in the Oldham job. I'm 28 and looking forward to coaching when I retire. Barring emigrating to Australia, there are not many clubs I'd leave Salford for in this country.' The story fizzled out and, today Chris dismisses it as another fabricated newspaper 'story' claiming 'I never said any of that! That was in

1973 before winning the Championship with Salford and touring again. Not a chance!'

Apart from appearing against Swinton at Station Road on 23 May – a testimonial match for their wonderful servant Ken Gowers – Salford's season came to an unexpected halt on Sunday afternoon, 29 April, in the opening round of the Championship play-off. The visitors, Rochdale Hornets, shocked the Reds by winning 14-10 in what was an entertaining match, although the only positive for Salford was Watkins kicking his 221st goal of the season, thereby eclipsing the world record of 219 – set by Oldham's Bernard Ganley in 1957/58.

McNamara's opening match report for the 1973/74 campaign gave the rugby league fraternity a 'Hesketh Warning' – an indication that Salford's dazzling centre was on course to continue his excellent form of the previous term. Those two words provided the stark headline preceding McNamara's verdict on the pre-season friendly with Dewsbury at The Willows on 3 August. Although not good news for Chris's opponents, it was exactly the fillip that the club's supporters required as the season began. Salford won 25-6 in a canter on a greasy, slippery surface, McNamara expanding by writing 'Salford centre Chris Hesketh took only half an hour to prove that he is one of the fittest and keenest men in rugby league – before the season has opened! Hesketh took an inside pass from stand-off Ken Gill in last night's friendly against Dewsbury, then sidestepped and swerved through the thinnest of gaps to score a glorious try. It would have been a notable effort at the peak of the season, let alone one before a ball has been kicked in anger.'

Salford added pace to their already quicksilver three-quarter line with the capture of England rugby union international wing, Keith Fielding, from the Birmingham-based Moseley club. Fielding joined the Red Devils in May 1973, following a month of intense press speculation on his impending switch to the 13-a-side game. It was to be an impressive first season by the flying wingman, his final try-tally for Salford of 46 – he also scored a further three on his Great Britain debut – surpassing Bob Brown's 40-year-old club record of 45:

Keith Fielding had blistering pace and you could never take that away from him. As I've said before, Maurice Richards wasn't pure pace, but he had a brilliant sidestep and could take on a couple of defenders, beat them and score. What we had to do with Keith was create the gap or the overlap for him. But if you gave it him in that situation it was all over with. Probably his defence wasn't his best asset and I must admit on one occasion I did say a few words to him when Castleford scored in his corner and shouldn't have done! But you could say that about a lot of players – league and union – and to be fair to Keith, you could be losing 10-8 with a minute a go and parked on your own line and, if you could work the overlap, all he needed was half a yard. You knew he could run the length of the field and nobody would get near him. Just think, we had Fielding on one wing and Richards on the other! It's not bad that is it?

Fielding made a try-scoring debut in the clubs second pre-season friendly on 10 August, an 18-15 win at St Helens. The match was used by Evans to experiment with Chris at stand-off and Ken Gill at scrum-half, a combination used in the second half of the earlier friendly with Dewsbury. Regular scrum-half Pete Banner had temporarily lost favour and been demoted to a substitute spot. The Hesketh–Gill partnership was preferred four times during August, an exception being the visit to Bramley on the 25th when Gill was reunited with Banner, Chris returning to the centre. When the interval arrived, however, a gritty Bramley side were on course for a shock result and, in an effort to turn things round, Evans moved Chris to stand-off again and Gill back to scrum-half. Salford eventually won 14-7, Chris having 'stepped into the picture with some commendable enterprise, splitting the home defence before sending Charlton racing through for the first try.' Chris recalled 'We were level 2-2 at half-time and Cliff Evans got Charlo and myself together and said "Chris, keep going to acting half-back and bring Paul into the line to break them down." It came off, and Paul scored a vital try. I wasn't as fast as Charlo, but I could pick the ball up, scoot away and pull the defence in. Charlo knew the ball was coming off my left shoulder and, thankfully, the game was ours.'

By September Chris had reverted to his more familiar position in the centre, Banner, who – although not listed – had come close to joining Oldham at the start of that month, resurrecting his alliance with Gill. With a settled line-up and one of the best back divisions in the history of the club, Salford began the season in great form, winning the opening nine competitive matches including a resounding 47-17 win over Doncaster at The Willows in the opening round of the Players' No.6 Trophy, Chris registering his third professional try hat-trick in the process. It was a winning streak that incorporated Salford earning a place in their second consecutive Lancashire Cup Final, whetting the fans' appetite for entertaining the Australians on 30 September, the opening match of their tour. The occasion provided spectacular entertainment for the 11,064 attendance, with Salford – playing their fourth match in eight days – losing to the Kangaroos 15-12 in what was, poetically, described as 'a defeat more memorable and magnificent than any of those victories.'

Two weeks later, on 13 October, Salford came unstuck again, losing 19-9 to Wigan in the Lancashire Cup Final at Warrington. Their conquerors, who were struggling with their form that season, pulled a shock result out of the hat, former Reds' favourite Peter Smethurst giving an inspired display for the Cherry and Whites. Outside of those hiccups, Salford continued to impress with their exciting brand of rugby, Brian Snape proudly declaring it the best Salford team since he took over as chairman. The League competition had been split into two divisions prior to the 1973/74 campaign and, by the end of October, the Red Devils led Division One with seven wins from seven matches.

During December, the Salford team was knocked out of its stride with two further setbacks. Firstly, they were well beaten in yet another cup match by Leeds, this time 17-4 at The Willows in the second round of the Players' No.6 Trophy. It was then announced that Evans had decided to step down as coach through ill health, having been feeling unwell for a while. He later took on the less demanding role of chief scout. His natural successor was Les Bettinson who, after taking control of the team on a caretaker basis, was confirmed as permanent replacement:

Les Bettinson was another very good coach. He always talked to you man-to-man and was very straightforward. Les is a very intelligent man who didn't need to shout and bawl. He had a more thoughtful, technical approach. I wouldn't say he was a 'Cliff Evans' and, in fact, Eric Ashton wasn't either – but there were not many Cliff Evans's knocking about! But you still had to work to a pattern and I think Les was very good at running through the moves with us. He was a little fortunate in that he had some good players around at the time but I'm not knocking his ability. He was – and still is – a total gentleman who, perhaps, never achieved all he would have liked to as a coach. He was a player at the club when I arrived – and a good one too – and he developed into an excellent, meticulous coach. Alan McInnes, who took over Les's previous role as trainer, was the same. These men had gone through college education and had been taught how to be like that. They knew the basics, and I think that's what came through with Les. Les was always a good coach on the training ground as well. We had very high fitness levels and always trained very hard at Salford.

Under Bettinson, the Red Devils continued to rack up victories in the race for the League title and even managed a rare triumph at Castleford, by 16-11, on 6 January. The following weekend, in an effort to ease a fixture backlog, it was decided to play two League games, both at home. On Saturday 12 January they beat a dogged Bramley – on paper the easier of the two matches – by only 14-10. With a tough looking fixture looming against Wakefield Trinity the next day, Chris was asked his views on having to play again so soon, responding 'It's no use moaning. We're a very fit outfit and should be able to play two matches in two days. It's the knocks you take in the first match that are the trouble in the second. Wakefield have a big pack and that could be the telling point tomorrow.' Thankfully for their supporters, Salford looked surprisingly unsullied and demonstrated far better form than they had 24 hours earlier in their 22-7 defeat of Trinity.

As a result of their weekend double, and with only one League defeat – at Warrington in late October – from their first 15 Championship fixtures, Salford led Division One, four points clear of St Helens. As the title would be awarded to whoever topped the final table – the play-offs having been abolished with the introduction of two divisions – the Reds were looking a good bet to win their first Championship since 1939. But a golden chance to raise the drawbridge further against their closest challengers was blown in the next match, on Sunday 27 January, when they lost 12-11 to St Helens at The Willows. Salford trailed 12-3 with only two minutes remaining when, in the words of Bearshaw, they 'almost pulled off an escape story to match anything that happened at Colditz.' Firstly, Richards got the Reds back into contention with a try, converted by Watkins, to cut the deficit to four points. Then, with seconds left on the clock, Dixon went over in the corner, Watkins just failing to land the difficult kick as the Saints survived for a dramatic victory.

Salford's next League fixture was also at home, on Sunday 10 February, when they struggled to break down a solid-looking

Widnes defence. The Reds were just 7-5 ahead during the first half when Watkins attempted a penalty shot at goal. Not wishing to break the habit of a lifetime, Chris followed up the ball, which was hooked wide of the posts, and, with a defender failing to gather cleanly, dashed over the try-line to get his hands on it and score. It was a vital touchdown, shaking Salford out of their lethargy to post a 19-7 win, keeping them two points ahead of St Helens in the table.

With the Reds playing as well as ever and enjoying their best League season since the 1930s, thoughts inevitably turned to Wembley. Could 1974 be the year at last? They had begun their glory bid in tremendous form, dazzling Oldham at The Willows on 3 February with six exciting tries, including two from Chris – who was deemed to be 'at his liveliest' – to win 26-12. Their 'reward' was a second round draw that the fans dreaded – a visit to Leeds on Saturday 23 February! In a bid to beat their 'hoo-doo', club officials provided subsidised coach travel at 40 pence return each in an effort to get as much vocal support inside Headingley as possible. The initiative worked with over 50 coaches containing more than 2,500 fans – described in one paper as 'rent-a-crowd' – departing from Willows Road in scenes reminiscent of Salford's 1969 Wembley excursion. But there was to be no happy ending for Salford, with Leeds – coached by Chris's former mentor Eric Ashton – just winning 10-6 to claim their seventh consecutive win over the Reds. Leeds, with two early tries, had led 10-2 at the interval and Chris, in his post-match verdict, ruefully gave credit to former Castleford scrum-half, Keith Hepworth, saying 'He continually ripped holes in our defence from acting half-back in the first 20 minutes.'

The cup exit meant that the Championship chase became Salford's main focus. The following three League fixtures were won, placing their next match – a mid-week visit to St Helens on Tuesday 19 March – firmly into the 'crucial' category. The two were still neck-and-neck at the summit, Salford retaining their two-point advantage, the clear objective for St Helens being the completion of a League 'double' to draw level. Billed as the 'match of the season' it lived up to its hype, the *Daily Mirror's* Jack Humphreys describing it as 'a thrill-a-minute show.' Chris, deputising at stand-off for Gill, involved in an accident at work earlier that day, had an outstanding game, although struggling with a knee injury. 'I remember that the match was something of a classic. I played with a hamstring pull which had been bothering me for a while' says Chris. 'I was having daily ultrasound treatment with a physiotherapist in John Street, Manchester, and someone at the club asked "You'll be all right for St Helens won't you?" How I got through that match I don't know!' But get through it he did, the resultant 19-19 draw preserving the status quo as far as the Championship situation was concerned.

Despite the psychological advantage that Salford gained by the outcome at Knowsley Road, the Saints were still title favourites in a lot of minds. The reason was not hard to fathom. The Reds had nine matches to go but, mostly due to earlier postponements, eight of them were away fixtures. In a frantic closing schedule – which included a run of seven matches in only 16 days – the Reds suffered four defeats. Salford had one match left; at Wigan on Easter Monday, 15 April. They began the day – which would be one of the most nerve-wracking in the history of the club – still leading the Division One table by just one point from St Helens. The Saints, however, had two games left.

Salford faced their destiny at Central Park on a hot, sunny afternoon, knowing a slip-up would be disastrous. It did not start well and their aspiration looked dead and buried 30 minutes from time, as Wigan led 12-5. It was Chris, who had worked so hard in defence to quell the Wigan hordes in the opening half, who sparked the revival. He broke through the heart of the Wigan cover to set up Richards for a try in the corner. The score lifted the spirits of a jaded Salford outfit who, summoning fresh reserves of stamina, ran in three more unanswered tries, clinching a sensational 21-12 victory. Salford captain Watkins admitted to Paul Harrison of *The Sun* that 'I honestly thought our Championship hopes had gone for good and when we were down 12-5, I was even more certain. But then Chris Hesketh told me Wigan were tired.' Harold Mather, in *The Guardian*, declared 'it would be difficult to imagine a better, more exciting match' whilst Bearshaw had no doubts about Chris's contribution, saying 'Chris Hesketh had a magnificent game against the club he joined 11 years ago. He stifled many Wigan assaults and made the try that started Salford on their second-half winning way.'

It was a tremendous match at Wigan and I remember that the forwards played particularly well that day. They got on top of Wigan's pack, which made it easier for the backs, giving us more room, especially in the second-half. The win completed a difficult Easter programme. We had played at Leigh and Oldham, who were both near the bottom of the table, and struggled, although I suppose they were both desperate for points to avoid being relegated. We went to Leigh on Good Friday and were losing 21-13 well into the second-half but managed to come back strongly late on. Maurice Richards got the winning try for us right at the end. Then on Saturday we were at Oldham and played terrible, really awful. Oldham beat us 4-2 and it looked as if we'd blown the Championship at that stage.

As exhilarating as the win was, the Salford contingent could not count on any of their chickens until the second-leg of the Easter Monday bonanza was completed. Three hours after the final whistle blew at Central Park, St Helens met Widnes and many of the Salford players, officials and fans travelled across to Naughton Park that evening to witness it. A defeat for St Helens meant the Championship prize was destined for Salford's trophy cabinet. In another nerve-tingling, nail-biting match for the Salford supporters, Widnes staged their own second half revival to win 12-9, chairman Snape declaring afterwards 'I don't think I've cheered as much for my own team as I did for Widnes tonight!'

Salford received their trophy before the following Sunday afternoon's home clash with Bradford Northern. Over 10,000 fans turned out to see club captain Watkins, Chris and the rest of the team parade the Championship trophy around The Willows for the first time in 35 years. But it was a case of 'After the Lord Mayor's Show' in the match that followed. In what was the opening round of the Club Merit Championship – a new supplementary competition designed to replace the redundant Championship play-off – Bradford held Salford 16-16, winning the replay at Odsal four days later by 17-8. Watkins, in excusing the defeat, said at the time 'We were still a very tired side. The final run-in to winning the Championship drained us completely.' The sudden, unexpected end to the season, though, could not detract from what had been a successful campaign for the Red Devils, who had thrilled crowds wherever they went with their spectacular style of fast, open rugby:

We were at the top of the table for most of the season, although we had only a small pool of players and had a few injuries. We lost Mike Coulman and Maurice Richards for several months at the start of the season, then Eric Prescott and Peter Walker were unavailable and, of course, Ken Gill missed five vital matches after his works accident during the final run in. But you have to give some credit for the success to the unsung heroes that played in the pack, like Graham McKay, Doug Davies and Alan Grice who worked really hard all season. It was wonderful that we were able to win the Championship for our supporters.

The start of a wonderful rugby league career! 10-year-old Chris, second left at back, with the St Cuthbert's school team.

All set for a game of rugby union in the colours of West Park Grammar School, St Helens, aged 14.

West Park Old Boys rugby union team in 1961/62. Chris, second left on the front row, was playing in an open age side despite passing only his 17th birthday during the season.

Wearing the cherry and white of Wigan. He joined his hometown club from the Orrell Colts rugby union team in 1963.

His first professional hat-trick! Chris scores against Hunslet at Central Park on 30 March 1963, as he enjoys a dream home debut for Wigan in a competitive fixture.

Wembley-bound in 1966. An all-star Wigan squad pose at Central Park just seven days ahead of their clash with St Helens. Chris is seated, extreme left.

With his Salford colleagues in 1967/68, his first season at The Willows. Chris is in the centre, kneeling. Next to him, with the ball, is skipper and fellow Wiganer, Jackie Brennan.

Scoring a spectacular try in the corner at Swinton, as Salford overcome their local rivals 19-3 during the 1969 Easter weekend.

On the way to a 'try' against Castleford at Wembley in May 1969, but referee Deryk Brown, extreme left, disallowed the score, claiming a 'double movement.'

Ouch! Chris feels the force of a collision against the Sydney Colts in Australia during the 1970 Great Britain tour.

Chris, middle row, second left, with the Great Britain 1970 World Cup squad, prior to the tournament taking place in England during the autumn.

Breaking through during the first Test against the 1971 New Zealand tourists at
The Willows on 25 September. Despite scoring a try, Chris found himself on the wrong
end of an 18-13 score-line.

Chris, with the ball, and the Lancashire team before a county championship fixture at Leigh, 29 September 1971. It was the first time he captained a professional side, although visitors Yorkshire sullied the occasion by winning 42-22!

The Salford team pose with the Lancashire Cup, having beaten Swinton 25-11 in the final at Warrington on 21 October 1972. It was the first major trophy success for Chris, seated, second left, and the first silverware for Salford since 1939.

World Champions 1972! Chris parades the coveted trophy with Salford team-mate Paul Charlton after Great Britain's extra-time thriller against Australia in Lyon on 11 November.

About to cross the line for a try against Oldham in the first round of the Rugby League Challenge Cup at The Willows on 3 February 1974. Salford won 26-12 but lost at Leeds in the next round. It was one of the biggest frustrations for Chris and his colleagues that they were unable repeat their 1969 Wembley visit.

Perfect balance as Chris prepares to off-load in a typical action shot.

Rugby League champions of 1973/74! Chris is seated fourth from left, next to club chairman, Brian Snape. Skipper David Watkins is seated centre.

The pinnacle of Chris's career; captain of the 1974 Great Britain touring team. He is seen here, seated in the centre of the front row, surrounded by the rest of his squad at the Sydney Cricket Ground.

A proud moment! Chris, followed by Paul Charlton and Roger Millward leads the Great Britain team out for the first Test against Australia at Lang Park, Brisbane, on 15 June 1974.

Chris queries the decision of Toowoomba-based referee Don Lancashire as he awards a penalty to Australia during the first Test, which the hosts won 12-6.

Colin Dixon chairs his triumphant skipper around the Sydney Cricket Ground after Great Britain had levelled the 1974 series with a dramatic 16-11 win over Australia on 6 July.

Attempting to break away during the third and deciding Test of the 1974 series against Australia at the Sydney Cricket Ground on 20 July. Despite a valiant effort Great Britain just went down by 22-18.

Better luck in New Zealand as Chris evades Kiwi full-back Warren Collicoat to score in the corner during the third Test at Carlaw Park, Auckland, on 10 August 1974. Great Britain's emphatic 20-0 victory clinched the series after losing the opening Test on the same ground two weeks earlier.

Not a care in the world! The Great Britain skipper relaxes during the 1974 tour at the Great Northern Hotel, Auckland.

Muddy but victorious! Chris keeps a tight grip on the BBC2 Floodlit Trophy whilst held aloft by Salford colleagues after the fiercely contested Final replay against Warrington at Wilderspool on 28 January 1975.

Chris demonstrates his athleticism during a Salford training session to the obvious amusement of team-mates!

We're almost there! John Butler jumps up with delight as Chris places a congratulatory arm around Mike Coulman after the giant prop had powered over for Salford's third try at Keighley in only the 18th minute. Salford eventually won 18-10 to clinch the 1975/76 championship in their last league match of the season.

It's ours! The Salford skipper beams with delight after his side had received the Rugby League Championship Trophy - at The Willows on 30 April 1976 - for the second time in three years.

Champions versus Challenge Cup winners! Chris helps St Helens captain Kel Coslett display the Premiership Trophy, which their two clubs were all set to contest on 22 May 1976 at Swinton. It was Coslett that retained his smile the longest, Salford losing 15-2.

Keith Macklin, the well-known television and radio commentator, presents David Watkins and Chris with their testimonial cheques, at The Willows Variety Centre in February 1979.

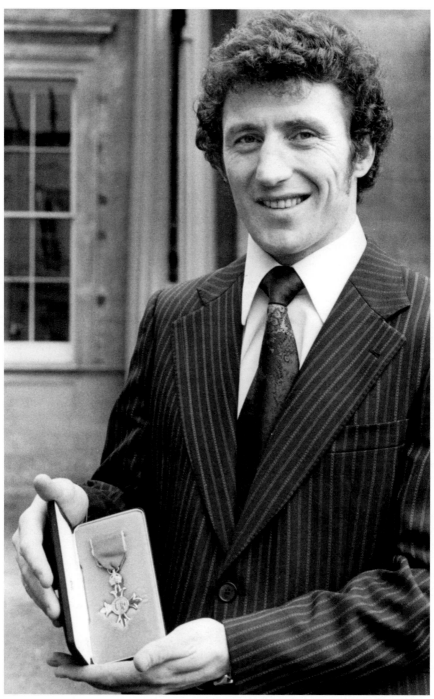

Chris shows off his MBE in the forecourt at Buckingham Palace after receiving his award from Her Majesty Queen Elizabeth II during February 1976, following his recognition in the New Years Honours List.

8

THE CLASS OF '74

Monday 4 March 1974 turned out to be one of the most significant dates in Chris's glorious rugby career. It was the day that Britain's international selectors chose the touring team that would depart for Australia and New Zealand in May. As widely predicted by the media, Chris claimed one of the 26 available places. But, there was a further announcement, that, temporarily at least, stunned Salford's star centre; his selection as tour captain. The first Wigan-born player to be accorded such a great honour, he admitted 'I didn't expect to go as captain at the time. I thought David Watkins, who was then our skipper at Salford, would be the captain.'

For several days after, Chris was living in a dream-like state, flooded by phone calls from well-wishers and letters of congratulation from near and far, with mail arriving from colleagues, supporters, rugby league officials and local businesses. It provided the icing on the cake in what was proving a momentous 1973/74 term for Chris. Salford was homing in on the Championship and, on a personal level, he had enjoyed his best-ever campaign in terms of representative honours. He had helped Lancashire overcome Cumbria 18-6 at Barrow on 5 September and – two weeks later – defeat Yorkshire in a tightly contested roses clash at Widnes by 17-15. The latter victory, which secured the county championship, was especially rewarding for Chris as he was chosen as team captain again, following a gap of two years.

Firmly established on the international scene, he was involved in all five of Great Britain's Test encounters during 1973/74: three against the touring Australians, two versus France. The rubber

113

with Australia gave Chris an unexpected return to Wembley, the prestige venue being chosen for the opening Test on Saturday 3 November. Unlike his first two visits – in 1966, when he remained on the bench as his Wigan colleagues were defeated, and 1969, when he was in Salford's beaten side – his 1974 appearance ended in victory. Watched by British Prime Minister, Ted Heath, the host nation won an exciting match 21-12, Chris being involved in the move that led to the opening try by Britain's second-row forward Phil Lowe in the fourth minute. The match – televised live, as was the whole series, by the BBC and switched from Wigan at the request of Australian officials – drew a disappointing attendance of just 9,874. Having previously opposed the Aussies in three World Cup clashes, the Wembley clash was Chris's first experience of competing in an Anglo-Australian Test.

The Kangaroos squared the series with a 14-6 triumph at Headingley three weeks later, their second-rower Bob McCarthy scoring the only try three minutes after the break. It was a match where both sides battled against a third opponent: a gale force wind. The decisive match was at Warrington's Wilderspool Stadium on Saturday 1 December, the elements throwing up arctic-like conditions for the two teams. On a freezing cold day, the protective straw covering laid earlier in the week failed to stop the pitch becoming granite-like and rutted, its dangerous looking icy surface being covered by braziers in a late bid to soften the worst sections. But for being televised it is probable that the game would have been postponed but, in the event, the visitors adapted better, winning the Test – and the series – 15-5. The Aussies inflicted most of the damage with four unconverted first half tries, one of which was by Bobby Fulton who, ironically, had been born in Warrington. The Lions' only try was a Roger Millward effort five minutes into the second period, Chris having been involved in an excellent move that led to the consolation touchdown:

I particularly remember that surface! Our studs were

clattering on it. It was that hard. But it was the same for both teams and it was disappointing to lose the series. At Wembley, it was nice to beat the Australians and come off a winner. We were all really made up about that. I think they expected to draw a lot of the Aussies who lived in London to the match and, to a certain extent, I suppose they did, but it certainly wasn't full. I think if the stadium had been full to the rafters it would have had more tension and been more of an occasion.

His next international calling – the two meetings with France – also proved to be a special event in Salford's history. Chris was one of six Salford players who were selected for both matches, a record representation from The Willows outfit, the others being Paul Charlton, Colin Dixon, Keith Fielding, Ken Gill and David Watkins. Consequently, ninety Salford supporters flew over to the Stade Municipal, Grenoble, for the first game, played on Sunday 20 January. France had led 5-3 when Chris was involved in a move – along with Gill, Dixon and Halifax centre Dave Willicombe – that led to Doug Laughton's try, the Widnes loose-forward's effort opening the floodgates for four more touchdowns; one by Gill and a hat-trick from Fielding, both making their Great Britain debuts. Chris, described as 'a defensive star' in one match report, paid a heavy price for the 24-5 victory. 'A French player tackled me so hard, he sprung my rib cage and it never ever went back again' explained Chris. 'For about a month afterwards it was the sorest thing I've ever known, sheer agony every time I breathed. For weeks I had to have tape strapped all round me really tight when I played for Salford.'

The return encounter, at Wigan's Central Park on Sunday 17 February, produced another emphatic win, this time by 29-0. Britain's players were motivated by the fact that the 1974 touring team was to be announced a few weeks later, many perceiving that the meetings with the French were being used as 'tour trials', Chris being one of several players named by *Manchester Evening News* correspondent Jack McNamara 'who enhanced their tour chances.'

The media also predicted Laughton, skipper in both Tests against France, was in pole position to lead the tourists. Interestingly, Laughton himself disputes that supposition, claiming in his fascinating biography *A Dream Come True* (London League Publications, 2003) that he was led to believe that was not the case. The truth, whatever it was, became irrelevant a few days after the Wigan Test when Laughton signed a contract which committed him to spend the 1974 close season in Australia – but playing for Sydney-based club Canterbury-Bankstown!

Speculation on the tour captaincy was immediately focused towards The Willows. Paul Hince, writing in the *Manchester Evening News* made the claim that 'David Watkins is favourite' citing that the Welsh star, who had led the British Lions in two rugby union Tests against the All Blacks in New Zealand during 1966, had 'all the right qualities required of a tour captain.' Hince went on to reveal, however, that 'One of his rivals for the job is likely to be his Salford team-mate Chris Hesketh. In fact, Hesketh gets the vote from his own chairman Brian Snape, who is a member of the Test selection committee.' Intriguingly, Snape – despite the fact that Watkins was the Salford club captain – was quoted as saying 'I think Chris has the best chance of the job.' Chris responded at the time to the guesswork by stating that 'the captaincy of a touring party to Australia is the top personal honour in the game. But I don't even consider myself having a tour place until I am picked.'

When Chris was confirmed as the committee's choice for leading the 1974 tour, the celebrations in Salford were stimulated by the news that the other five Reds players that had appeared against France were also in the party. It was a record contribution by the club, beating the previous high of five that had taken part in the 1936 expedition. Watkins, himself elated at being chosen for the squad, said 'My hopes for Great Britain's success are geared to the fact that my club-mate Chris Hesketh is the tour skipper. If ever a player deserved to get the maximum accolades from the game it is Chris. He has spared himself no effort to reach the top and, with the kind of support he will get from his men, I am confident he can bring back the Ashes.'

Fielding announced, a few days after his selection, that he was standing down because his wife was expecting their first child and because of his commitment to a new teaching job in Cheshire, having recently transferred following his signing by Salford. The Red Devils' contingent was later restored to six when Maurice Richards flew out in early July as a replacement for injured Leeds wingman John Atkinson. Atkinson had been one of only four players to survive from the 1970 tour party, the others being Hull Kingston Rovers half-back Roger Millward, Featherstone Rovers forward Jim Thompson and Chris himself. Thompson had made the cut as a pre-tour replacement for unlucky Warrington packman Mike Nicholas, whose injury in the Challenge Cup Final at Wembley forced him to withdraw. Chris considered Thompson to be a very worthwhile addition to the squad:

Jimmy Thompson was a fantastic defensive player, the best tackling machine I've ever come across. As far as I was concerned, you could have all the flyers in the world in your team but if you're not tackling you don't win. That is rugby league. If they don't score, we don't lose. That's how you start off. It's very boring I know, but the first thing to do is stop them scoring. Then, when you've got players outside you like Charlton, Watkins and Atkinson, you can 'murder' them.

The excitement of his captaincy of the touring side and the euphoria associated with Salford clinching the Championship kept Chris fairly busy in the days before departing Manchester Airport for Darwin. He told one journalist: 'Naturally I'm very proud as a Wigan-born lad. I'm feeling a little shattered with all the receptions I've been attending as the new British captain and with Salford after the winning of the League title. But I'm not complaining – it's when people stop inviting me that I suppose I'll start worrying. I think this tour squad will give a good account of themselves, although some folk criticise the choice – but I think they'll be giving 100 per cent effort to try and bring the Ashes back to England. I've said before that I think this is going to be a tour squad which will surprise a few people.'

Although his 1974 Lions would not, ultimately, reclaim the Ashes given up to the Aussies following the 1973 series defeat in England, Chris and his charges were to enjoy a successful and eventful tour. Managed by Blackpool Borough director Reg Parker and coached by St Helens' Jim Challinor, the tourists experienced all the usual highs and lows associated with such a lengthy trip, with a few controversial moments thrown into the mix for good measure. All guaranteed to keep journalists in both hemispheres occupied and happy!

After arriving in Australia, Chris soon realised the attention focused on him by the Aussie press would multiply ten-fold compared to the British media. The headline in their *Rugby League Week* magazine previewing the tour read 'English Skipper After Aussie Blood.' Written by English rugby league journalist Brian Batty it began: 'Chris Hesketh possesses the build and profile of a middleweight boxing champion, the heart of a lion and a burning desire to lead Great Britain to success in their bid to regain The Ashes.' It went on to warn Antipodean readers – and probably a few of their players as well – that 'The superbly-fit Salford centre has a reputation for being the game's hardest tackler pound for pound.'

The tourists won their first five matches, played against district teams in the Northern Territories and Queensland, by comfortable margins, although not considered to be firing on all cylinders at that early stage. One report even described the British side as 'lethargic.' The sixth match provided a much sterner contest, facing Queensland at Lang Park, Brisbane, on Sunday 9 June, watched by the biggest crowd so far – 20,274. In what was Chris's fifth appearance of the tour, his side sneaked home 13-12, a drop-goal by Featherstone Rovers scrum-half Steve Nash proving the deciding factor.

Six days later, Lang Park hosted the first Test, and Australian Prime Minister Gough Whitlam was amongst the crowd of 30,280. In a match that most critics felt was lacklustre, Chris and his Welsh wing partner, Warrington's John Bevan, almost grabbed the opening try, the pair giving chase to a ball that was trickling towards the Australian dead-ball line, just failing to get the vital touch. Subsequently, Australian winger Warren Orr scored the only try of the match just before half-time to give his country a lead of 7-2 at the interval. With the tourists being hit by injuries to their pack – particularly Featherstone hooker Keith Bridges and St Helens back-row George Nicholls – Chris moved to loose-forward in the second half, having what Parker later described as 'an outstanding game.' It was Chris that put his Salford colleague Paul Charlton through a gap, Graeme Langlands managing to haul the Cumbrian down at the last gasp when a try was threatening. But the Australians stood firm to win 12-6. Most journalists – particularly the British contingent that had travelled with the party to cover the tour – felt the match had been there for the taking by the visitors. 'I would agree with that' says Chris, 'and it would have been a massive start for us to have won the first Test. It was aggravating that we only lost by six points. Injuries depleted us in the forwards and it wasn't a bad Australian pack with Ron Coote, Arthur Beetson and Bob O'Reilly. It was a hell of a team that they put out and we'd had quite a few injuries on the tour already. And their press were giving us a bit of pain as well!'

The most infamous match of the tour occurred on Wednesday 26 June when the tourists travelled to Wade Park, Orange, in New South Wales to play a Western Division representative side. The result – 25-10 to Great Britain – was almost irrelevant as Chris came within a whisker of creating headline news by leading his team off the field and back to the dressing room, an action that would have reverberated around the rugby-playing world. It was a match now remembered as 'The Battle of Orange.'

Now that was a dirty game believe me! Hardest match I played in? No! Dirtiest? Yes! Reg Parker agreed with me to the point where we nearly took the team off the field. Straight from the kick off there were elbows going in, short arms, trip tackles – the lot! We were winning all the way – I don't think we were ever behind but I had to go to the referee eventually. Two or three of their players went in on somebody and I said to the ref 'Hold on a minute mate!' But he didn't give us anything. I said 'Somebody's going to get badly hurt here if you don't send them off.' And the ref – I can't remember who he was but he obviously wasn't a good ref – he said 'I'm in charge of this game, go away' and I said 'Well I'm the captain and I'm telling you this is dangerous.' Then it got really mad and I went over to the bench and said to Reg 'If this carries on I'm taking them off because somebody's going to get killed.' It would have been a staggering thing if I had done that. It would have been on all the news bulletins. They were infuriating our lads to the point it was making our lads go back at them, because you're bound to do, and he was just penalising us all the time. The crowd was giving it plenty as well – it was very hostile. Reg said 'It's nearly half-time, let's get the team back in the dressing room and try and calm things down a bit.' I think Reg was going to try and have a word with the referee during the break, although, eventually four players got sent off, two from each side.

Even the Australian sports press were horrified at the spectacle they had witnessed. The writer in the *Central Western Daily* said 'While Wednesday's rugby league match between Great Britain and Western Division was a tremendous financial success, Orange League officials have expressed bitter disappointment at the conduct of players and spectators. While local officials were elated at the financial success they were very quick to add their total disapproval at the disgraceful incidents which took place on and off the field.' Mick Noonan, who was chairman of the organising committee for what, to them, was a prestige fixture said 'The committee has worked hard for weeks to make this game a success, all the hard work went down the drain in 100 minutes of the most disgraceful football and crowd behaviour I have ever seen.' Another Australian official was quoted as saying 'I feel the Englishmen were almost blameless, as they had gone onto the field with the intention of playing football, but had been bashed from pillar to post in a disgraceful exhibition. I would have been in full agreement with the English captain Chris Hesketh leading his players off the field when he wanted to. Wednesday's match at Wade Park is now being mentioned in the same category as the famous "Battle of Brisbane" in 1958.' 'The after-match reception was very cool. We went to it but their officials were slightly embarrassed' recalls Chris.

Another stern task – although of a less malicious nature – awaited the tourists three days later at Sydney Cricket Ground when they faced New South Wales. 'I think one of the hardest matches on the tour is against New South Wales. It is a very tough match, almost like another Test match against what is virtually a Test strength team' says Chris. Britain's injury ravaged side battled manfully in losing 13-9 but suffered further blows when Warrington hooker Kevin Ashcroft and Oldham prop Terry Clawson were added to the casualty list. Both eventually returned to action after being sidelined for almost a month, an SOS being sent home in the meantime for Bradford Northern prop Bill Ramsey to be flown out to bolster the troops.

The highpoint of the Australian leg of the tour – and one of the most rewarding moments in Chris's entire rugby league career – was undoubtedly the second Test at Sydney Cricket Ground. Already one down in the series, with a crippling injury list – only 17 fit players necessitating final team selection late at night on the eve of the match – they were not considered by the Aussie press to have 'clicked' as a team. That latter perception changed dramatically on the afternoon of Saturday 6 July.

The injury woes meant some dramatic team changes, some tactical and some patching up the holes left by the wounded. In the former category was the key decision, taken several days before the Test, to call up Gill at stand-off in place of Millward as partner to Nash. In the latter category was the decision to put Millward on one wing, Leeds centre Les Dyl on the other, and St Helens full-back David Eckersley in the centre, Chris being the only player appearing in the three-quarter line in his usual position. In the pack, with two first choice hookers injured, third ranked John Gray – who had joined Wigan from Coventry Rugby Union Club a year earlier – was called up, second-rower Thompson filling the demanding role of blind-side prop.

Displacing Millward at stand-off was a move that shocked the Australian media. The Aussies team manager, Charlie Gibson, quoted in the Australian daily, *The Sun*, on the Thursday before the Test, asked 'What has he done wrong? Everyone is saying what a poor team they are but the one doubt I have now is just how good is their backline if they can dispense with Millward. It might be time to take another look at their prospects.' The reason for their angst was that Millward, who had made a big impression with the 1970 party, was a big favourite Down Under, whereas Gill was relatively unknown before the tour.

In the same edition of *The Sun*, under the headline 'Salford To The Rescue', journalist EE Christensen attempted to provide some answers, explaining 'Great Britain in Saturday's second Test will use moves which took Salford to this years English Championship. This is one of the main reasons for the inclusion of Salford's five-eighth Ken Gill at the expense of Roger Millward. Salford will have centre Chris Hesketh and full-back Paul Charlton in Saturdays Test as well as second-rower Colin Dixon. Tour manager Reg Parker says that with Charlton joining in so many moves it will be an advantage to have Gill directing the backline play. "Salford is the best team in England and Gill is the man who calls the play for the backline" said Mr Parker. "He was ranked ahead of Millward when we left home, but Roger, of course, is a very smart player and I know how highly he is rated here. The Australian fans will appreciate Gill after they see him operating in a Test team" Mr Parker added.' Great Britain's team was: Charlton, Dyl, Eckersley, Hesketh, Millward, Gill, Nash, Mills, Gray, Thompson, Dixon, E Chisnall, Nicholls. Substitutes: Norton, A Bates.

Parker was spot-on in his prediction. McNamara, covering the epic encounter in Sydney for the *Manchester Evening News*, wrote: 'The miracle has happened – injury stricken Great Britain beat Australia 16-11 to level the series in a brilliant and courageous display. They beat the cocky Aussies with thrilling attacking football, inspired by halves Steve Nash and Ken Gill.' Things did not look so rose-coloured early on, however, after Bobby Fulton, watched by a 48,000 crowd, touched down in the corner in only the 9th minute to give the hosts a 3-0 lead. Four minutes later a brawl erupted as a scrum was about to be formed, Gray being forced to leave the field for 12 minutes to have a massive gash over his left eye patched up. It was then that Britain, with their temporary numerical disadvantage, showed their grit, doggedly denying the Australians any chance of increasing their score. After Gray returned, Britain put their foot on the gas to blitz the Australians with three tries in an eight minute purple patch – all under the posts and converted by Gray – from Chisnall (36th minute), Dixon (39th – Chris bursting through in support to provide the final pass) and Gill (44th). Gray provided the killer touch with a 51st minute drop-goal for a 16-3 lead. Australia came back with two tries in the last ten minutes but it was a case of too little too late and the day belonged to Britain – and their beaming and proud skipper, Chris.

The Great Britain leader woke up on Sunday morning to discover his name was dominating the Australian sports pages. One report, attributed to Chris himself as a guest writer, proclaimed 'The best is yet to come. We've been on the floor in recent weeks and yesterday's climb back up was just mighty. It's the bravest effort I've been associated with on a football field.'

Highly respected rugby league historian Robert Gate, in his book *The Struggle For The Ashes* (1986), described their display as 'one of the gutsiest performances by a British XIII in modern times.' *Open Rugby* magazine editor, Harry Edgar, in a 1979 retrospective, claimed 'Chris Hesketh had led his men to a sensational triumph, one to be chalked up alongside the history-making deeds of Wagstaff's "Rorke's Drift" in 1914 or Prescott's "Battle of Britain" at Brisbane in 1958.'

It was a wonderful feeling leading the team in a Test match particularly at the Sydney Cricket Ground. Even if it's full it seems strange because it's so big and the crowd are quite a bit of a way off. You emerge from this very old changing room and you think about who must have sat in there over the years, rugby league greats like Jim Sullivan and Gus Risman and famous cricketers such as Don Bradman – absolutely wonderful! When you walk around the place beforehand and you look at it, you can smell the history, it reeks of it.

The second Test was one of the proudest moments of my career. I didn't normally watch the clock but I can still remember now the clock inside the ground ticking down towards the end of the match and saying to the referee 'How long is left?' and he wouldn't tell me! There was one journalist who was saying before the second Test 'This Britain side will get mopped up and the Aussies will beat them by 20 points.' He'd had a real go at us. And, of course, we won the match – a brilliant effort by everybody and I mean everybody – and afterwards I came walking off the field saying 'Where's this journalist now? Where is he?'

Two weeks later, in the same historical setting of Sydney's famed cricket ground, 55,505 spectators poured through the turnstiles to see the third and decisive Test. As in the previous encounter, Australia got off to a flier with a 9th minute 3-0 lead through a Lionel Williamson try. In the 18th minute Britain responded to go ahead 5-3 after Chris was brought down inches from the try-line having supported a Charlton break, Dyl somehow squeezing over the line from the resultant play-the-ball and Gray converting. A further penalty to each side took it to 7-5 for the Lions when, in the 27th minute, Chris believes the match and the series was won and lost, when, with Britain looking certain to score, Bob McCarthy intercepted a Gill pass to race over virtually unopposed. Langland's conversion put the Australian's 10-7 ahead instead of trailing 12-5. Britain did manage to mount a fight back, leading 16-10 at the interval – Maurice Richards having scored in the corner after capitalising on Ray Branighan mis-fielding a towering kick from the inspirational Gray – but Britain's pack tired after the resumption, Australia adding two further tries to win 22-18:

> The third Test was lost on one intercepted pass. I can see it now. We were going up the touchline. I gave the ball to Kenny Gill and Kenny fired a pass to the wing. Bob McCarthy intercepted the pass and went under the sticks. We had something like a three to two overlap. Don't get me wrong, I'm not blaming Gilly at all because that's what happens sometimes. But that's what lost us the third Test – one pass. If that pass had gone to the winger, I'm sure we would have scored and we'd have won the Test and we'd have won the Ashes. I think the result was disappointing because we'd hyped ourselves up to such a degree in the second Test and put two fingers up to the people who were knocking us. Even though we had injuries and a battered set of forwards who had played a lot of games, we weren't swamped by the Aussies. In three Tests against them in their own country, to lose by an overall total of five points is not a bad effort.

Just seven days later on Saturday 27 July, after licking their wounds, the patched-up and weary tourists – having flown over the Tasman Sea – took on New Zealand at Auckland's Carlaw Park. In what was the opening Test of another three-match series, the men in black won 13-8 on a mud-bath of a pitch, the Lions registering just two tries; from Nash – set up by a sidestep straight out of the top drawer from Chris – and Bevan. Apart from the obvious disappointment of losing, the biggest letdown was the refereeing of John Percival, which, from the viewpoint of the British contingent was on a par with their experience in Orange a month earlier. In a match that boiled over several times – the first brawl occurred in the 13th minute – Percival penalised the tourists 22 times! The British pack also suffered through the loss of Thompson – withdrawn from the fray after being concussed in a tackle – and Dixon, who was dismissed in the 59th minute for an alleged high tackle, although some reports claimed that – due to the players being caked in mud – the wrong man was sent off! Either way, it left the tourists short-handed for the last 20 minutes.

Fortunes changed dramatically for the two remaining Tests, Britain taking the series through two superb victories and Chris playing a true captains part as a stand out player in both. Peter Yaxley took charge of the second Test – staged at the Addington Show Grounds in Christchurch on Sunday 4 August – and, like his predecessor, favoured the home nation in his interpretation of the rules, New Zealand benefiting from a 16-4 penalty count. 'They can't all be Holy Ghost's and we can't all be sinners' was Chris's considered retort after the match. This time, though, on a much drier pitch, the Brits coped with that adversity much better, helped in part, by their re-familiarisation with the four-tackle rule. Although dispensed with in favour of six by Australia in 1971 and Britain in 1972, the New Zealanders still operated with a system that resulted in what was sometimes referred to as 'panic-rugby.'

McNamara, lavish with his praise of the tourists' skipper, wrote: 'Chris Hesketh, Great Britain's captain, had his finest game of the tour in yesterday's exciting 17-8 win in the second rugby league Test over New Zealand in Christchurch. Hesketh, playing at stand-off instead of centre because of injuries to Ken Gill and Roger Millward, thrived on being so involved in the action. He played with supreme authority, spurring the attack and marshalling the defence like a field commander in full control of a situation that had its moments of peril. As a backs to the wall effort it was a victory to cherish.' The high penalty count helped the Kiwi's full-back, Warren Collicoat, kick his side into a 6-0 lead after only 16 minutes play. Inspired by Chris, Britain rallied to go in 7-6 ahead at the break, Les Dyl having followed up his own kick to score the only try of the first period. There was some concern in the visitors camp when Charlton had to quit with a hamstring problem in the 59th minute, scrum half Nash going to full-back to cover the loss, being replaced by Alan Bates as Chris's new half-back partner. Ten minutes later, Collicoat regained the lead for New Zealand with his fourth penalty. Instead of crumbling, Britain's disrupted line-up dug deep and scored two late tries, through David Redfearn and Chris, who rounded off a good days work by retrieving a loose ball and sidestepping his way over the whitewash in the final seconds. According to one local journalist, Chris 'gave one of the finest displays seen by a stand-off in New Zealand for many years.'

The deciding Test was held the following weekend on Saturday 10 August, when a patched up Britain – who could only count on 13 fit players two days before the match – again met the Kiwis at Carlaw Park. As with the first Test, the pitch was a mud-heap, but of greater concern to the British camp was that Percival had again been appointed as referee. Parker and Challinor – accompanied by Chris – attended a meeting of the New Zealand League authorities during the week before the match to put their point of view. 'Percival had hammered us with penalties in the first Test' says Chris. 'We had a meeting with him, and some of the New Zealand officials, and it was very amicable. Reg was saying to Percival "You've penalised us for things we don't understand" and I know that every time I turned round and looked at him he'd got his hand up for a penalty! That made life very hard for us because they were getting free kicks, which took them into our half all the time. He did say that he would talk to our team, and did so, before the third Test.'

Despite that cordial dialogue, Percival still penalised Britain heavily in the third Test: 16 times with the Kiwis being pulled up on just four occasions! But the match, crucial as it was, was fought out in a better spirit than the previous two encounters, both of which had been niggling affairs littered with bouts of fisticuffs. Chris, who according to one New Zealand journalist 'made his mark on the game', again operated at stand-off. The Lions effectively won the match in the first half when, despite the tricky conditions underfoot, their superior speed and guile helped build up an 8-0 lead. It came on the back of two spectacular tries in the space of three minutes. The first – which opened the scoring – fell to Chris. New Zealand's *Sunday Herald* writer, Kevin Savage, described the action: 'After 20 minutes of stirring play by both sides, Hesketh found a gap 35 yards out, sprinted clear, cleverly caused Collicoat to hesitate slightly on the lookout for the infield sidestep, then burst away again very fast to the corner. This was a grand try and so was the sideline conversion by John Gray to give the tourists a 5-0 lead.' Moments later, Dyl made a lightning break to set up the second try, again scored in the corner, this time by Bevan.

The conditions deteriorated in the second half as heavy rain fell, the ground once more being converted into a treacle patch, creating a virtual stalemate for much of the last 40 minutes. Britain, though, capitalised on stray passes to intercept for two long distance breakaways tries by Dyl and Bevan, the final result being a comfortable, series clinching 20-0 scoreline. Robert Jones, writing in the local *8 O'Clock Liftout Sport* paper, revealed 'British skipper Chris Hesketh said he adopted a cautious approach early and pointed out the Kiwis could have been more dangerous if they'd scored first. But he added once Britain got on the scoreboard, and the mood that his lads were in, meant he could tell them to "play English-style football" and the response came.'

The *Auckland Star's* Brian Doherty declared 'This was the truest Test match of this Pall Mall series. It had none of the unpleasantness of the first two and none of the arguing. Instead Britain played football. It was tightly reined by Chris Hesketh, who, before the start of the game, made "peace offerings" of British pennants to (New Zealand captain) Ken Stirling and referee John Percival. Hesketh did a great job for Britain. He controlled his team and the play masterfully and, unlike the Kiwis, made certain his backs had their chances. Finally, the game owed much to referee Percival. He received a fair deal from the players and gave one back. Consequently, there was a true Test won by the best team. Who could ask for more except a better ground? The crowd was officially estimated at 22,000.'

Carlaw Park was a mud-bath, which was a leveller for everybody, and – I've got to be honest – it used to stink! And, yes, I did give a British pennant to John Percival! We took quite a few on tour and there were certain matches where we did give them out. I got a lot of satisfaction out of beating New Zealand. It has a small population but it is a big rugby country. They love their sport and they obviously love their rugby, probably union over league where, obviously, the All Blacks are the kings, but you felt appreciated. It is a beautiful country and they treated us right. They were wonderful hosts – as were the Australians – and we went to see all the traditional things that you associate with New Zealand. I made some great friends there as well. But, I have to say, we were all ready for going home at that stage and I can remember that a few of the lads were crossing the days off the calendar!

For Chris, though, the third Test against the Kiwis – which would have made a fitting climax – was not quite the final curtain.

Three days later – on Tuesday afternoon 13 August – he was back at Carlaw Park for the closing match against the Auckland provincial side. It was Chris's 20th appearance in a 28-match itinerary that had covered eleven hectic weeks, small wonder the weary tourists lost 11-2. The journey home, which began the next day, suffered long delays, the aircraft being stranded in Beirut after the Turkish invasion of Cyprus on 20 July had thrown the Middle East into a confused state. After travelling for over 40 hours they eventually landed at London's Heathrow Airport before catching a flight to Manchester. Chris returned to England feeling weary but exhilarated, having brought back with him a treasure-trove of memories, particularly of colleagues that shared the adventure with him:

Stevie Nash stood out for me – he was a wonderful tourist. In the second Test against Australia, the Aussies whacked this ball up in the air towards the sticks. I was running back to try and cover and Nash stood on the try line under the posts as two big Australian forwards were zooming in at him – and that ball was somewhere next to Mars! Nashy just stood there thinking to himself 'You've got to catch it' and I was trying desperately to get in between these two Aussies but they 'pin-balled' him. He caught the ball and 'smack!' – they hit him hard and he went back over the dead ball line! I just went up to him and said 'Bloody well done!' That was really brave. He never flinched and he was so wide open that if he'd fumbled it they would have scored.

Kenny Gill had a good tour as well. For me, Kenny came of age on that tour and he became a very, very good stand-off, albeit creative rather than incisive. You couldn't give Kenny the ball 80 yards out and expect him to run it in like Alex Murphy could or Shaun Edwards – he had a different, but very effective, style. I also thought my Salford colleagues Colin Dixon and Paul Charlton had very good tours. Charlo – who I roomed with for most of the tour – was supreme.

Jim Mills too! He was a fierce lad on the field, and he used to do some daft things, but he was a cracking bloke off it. We used to have some good singsongs with Jim. I remember on one occasion, Jim Challinor and Reg Parker and myself were having breakfast. We had injury problems and were discussing who would play in the match against Newcastle that coming weekend. Millsie – who had played in the previous Saturday's second Test against Australia and then the mid-week match at Wagga Wagga, against Riverina – was sat at the next table. All of a sudden he just looked up and said 'I'll play!' Reg Parker said 'No. You're not playing, Jim. You need a rest.' And Millsie, clearly very determined, just said 'I'll so-and-so play.' And he did! And we won! That's the sort of player Jim Mills was.

Being the captain of the 1974 Great Britain touring party provided Chris with the experience of a lifetime. He took pride in the fact that he was the first Wigan-born player to do so, and, as a Salford player, was proud of being the third tour captain provided by the club, following James Lomas in 1910 and Gus Risman in 1946:

The thing about being captain of a tour team is you've got responsibility and you've got to behave yourself. You've got to speak at endless functions and after a match they'd ask the British captain to say a few words and you've got to be able to do it. One thing that helped was that in most of my working life as a sales manager I've had to speak in front of people. I don't know where it comes from, but in my job I've always been involved with teams, and 'team building', and so on. I'm not an 'after-dinner' speaker, though. I'm not funny but, if it's about business and I've got to tell you how the years gone so far, or why we've done this or we're going to do that, I can do all that, and still drop the odd joke in now and again to break it up. But, if somebody said to me 'Will you come and speak at this dinner?' I would die! If they said 'We'll give you £500' I'd say 'You could give me £5,000 but I'm not doing it!' And, to be honest, every match I ever played in, I was always nervous before I went on the field but I always knew that once we kicked off I settled.

It's not easy on tour. Touring was very, very hard. The Aussies are big and strong and you have to play against them a couple of times a week and you're getting lambasted in the papers. Tours are also complicated, people-wise. Some players cry, some sulk, and some will go walks for hours on their own because they're really homesick. I was a bit homesick in my first tour in 1970 and, worse still, my dad died, but in the 1974 tour I was always busy being captain. I remember once they had me on television at about 8 o'clock in the morning and they sent a taxi to the hotel to collect me at 6 o'clock – things like that happened a lot. Rugby league's very big in Australia so you're in the public eye all the time and the media was always looking for angles. I remember once some journalists brought a large toy lion and a large toy kangaroo into the Coogee Bay Hotel in Sydney, where we were staying, and wanted a picture of me pulling the kangaroo's tail. I thought it was a bit stupid really and I refused to do it. I didn't want to be accused of animal cruelty even if it wasn't real!

Being captain was quite demanding in other ways too. You're on tour with 20-odd people for three months, with hotels, coaches, flying – it can be quite a strain. And also, you have the worry of 'Will we win the next match? Have we got enough fit players?' There are all sorts of things like that to consider. I would sit down with Reg Parker and Jim Challinor on occasions to pick the team for the next match. What you'd find yourself saying in a lot of cases was things like 'He's not fit and it's not your position, but will you play full-back or will you play loose forward?' In New Zealand, we had to play South Island at Greymouth and we were really struggling to put out a team and Jim Challinor played – and he scored a try!

There are some lads who go on tour and play their games and that's it, which is fair enough. But as captain you need some lieutenants in your side as well. You need two or three people who you can rely on, who can help take a bit of weight off your shoulders – and it is weighty being captain. You train every day. You've got the press every day. You might win, lose or draw, and for the next match you have to get them together and say 'Remember there's a lot of people at home looking to us and hoping we're going to carry it through. They're all in bed at the moment but we're going out there and we're going to do it for them.' We were a very good tour party in 1974 – very ordinary lads who were brilliant rugby players and many of them had to play out of position. I played all over as well but it doesn't matter if you can accomplish what you've got to do. It was, without a doubt, the highlight of my career – the fact that I could walk around and say 'I don't care how good or bad or indifferent I was as a player, but I captained Great Britain on a tour to Australia and New Zealand.' We didn't win the Ashes on the 1974 tour but it was a very successful tour.

At the conclusion of their long journey, Reg Parker said of his captain 'He has not only done his own job but organised everything as well' whilst one report said 'As skipper, Chris Hesketh was a sparkling success. His farewell speech at the end of the Australian tour was described by an Aussie journalist as the best-ever by a British skipper.'

9

TAKING THE REINS

Although he had led his country and county into battle on a rugby field, Chris had not given any thought to taking over the reins at The Willows on his return from the 1974 tour. Events, however, dictated that he was about to wrest the club captaincy from the grip of colleague David Watkins, skipper since 1968. Watkins who, by then, was travelling from South Wales each week to play, had already announced his intention to retire in the 1974/75 mid-season during December. Events overtook him, though, when he returned from the 1974 tour incapacitated. Having suffered a knee injury in Brisbane, he broke down completely in the opening match in New Zealand against North Island, tearing his knee ligaments and, although not realised at the time, sustaining a fracture above the knee. It was only natural that Chris, with his vast experience, would take command in Watkins' absence when the 1974/75 season began, an arrangement that became permanent when the Welshman announced his retirement a few months later, during October.

Chris had several matters on his mind following his return from the Antipodes. Being a rugby league tourist to Australia and New Zealand pushes players into the 'shop window' and, with Chris having the high profile associated with being tour captain, the media had a speculative field day – both Down Under and in Britain – as to which clubs he was expected to join. Reports emanating from Australia indicated there was interest from big Sydney clubs like Parramatta, Cronulla-Sutherland and Eastern Suburbs and from Queensland League outfits, Rockhampton and

Maryborough. The New Zealand rumour mill had him down for spending the 1975 British summer as a player–coach either in Wellington, Christchurch or Auckland.

Rockhampton had, reportedly, offered '£4,000 a year, plus playing wages' with Chris quoted, at the time, as saying 'The Rockhampton deal seemed quite fair, they were prepared to lay everything on for me, like a house, a job and a car.' Parramatta had also made overtures to Salford full-back Paul Charlton to join them and he and Chris had travelled home with contracts to sign for the 1975 close-season break. Salford had, apparently, told the Australian club they wanted £5,500 to release the pair on a short-term contract. Of greater concern to Salford fans was a report in *The Sunday People* by John Robinson that they could be about to lose their star centre for good as Chris was, apparently, seriously considering his retirement as a player. According to the report, he said 'I feel that I am at the crossroads and retirement is one of several avenues open to me. I am thinking seriously of whether I should give up the game for good or seek a position as a coach. I have also had a number of offers to join Australian clubs, which have to be considered. Whether I sign the (Parramatta) contract or not is another matter, but if I agree to go then next season will definitely be my last in English Football.'

Despite that report, I don't think I would seriously have retired at the end of that season. To be honest, I don't actually remember saying that but I might have been caught in a weak moment when I was still feeling a bit worn out after the tour. There was a lot of paper talk and speculation about offers that I had supposedly received. No person from New Zealand came to see me and ask me to join them. These stories just happen. On one occasion, at a hotel we were staying at, I had my picture taken in my tracksuit for an Auckland newspaper. They asked me things like 'Where do you work? What do you do for a living? Have you ever fancied going into coaching?' I'll reply 'Well yes, rugby league's been my life, but then I've also got another job as well that pays my mortgage.' Rugby league never paid my mortgage and never would do in my time. Then they asked 'Would you ever consider coming back to New Zealand?' and I would have said something very respectful like 'It's a beautiful country and I really would love to come back here.' The next day in their newspaper, you'd see 'Hesketh's going to sign for so-and-so.' That's how they do it to you. The only New Zealand approach I ever had came from Wellington in 1972. I was interested at the time, but decided against it. I think Wigan's Bill Francis went instead.

The only serious approaches I had on the 1974 tour were from Rockhampton, which, to be truthful, I was not really interested in, and from Parramatta. I've got the contract from Parramatta still. I think myself and Paul Charlton would have gone just for the summer. I can't remember now exactly why we didn't, but somehow it fell through. I believe there was a rule restricting the New South Wales clubs to a maximum of 13 imported players between them, which may have been a stumbling block. There again, you start saying to yourself 'That means going back to England and coming back here to Australia and playing again' and you're feeling battered. What you've got to remember is that clubs are talking to you all the time while you're on tour but, then, you get home and you're playing a full season again and feeling drained. All of a sudden you think to yourself 'Hold on a minute, do I want to fly out there again with my kids and all the upheaval – and play very hard rugby as well at the other end of the world?' You start to think 'I need a rest!'

His immediate destiny resolved, Chris turned his attention to the 1974/75 season and the task of leading Salford in defence of their Championship crown. It would prove a difficult commission.

Several of their tourists – including Chris himself – were jaded from over a year of non-stop rugby and, apart from Watkins, play-maker Ken Gill – also injured on tour – was absent for much of the season. The writing was on the wall when they travelled to Keighley for the opening fixture on 25 August. Despite disrupting their regular line-up through the use of back-row forward Colin Dixon as a stand-in centre and Chris taking over the stand-off berth once again, the Reds were strongly fancied to beat a team just promoted in third place from Division Two. The reality was that an enthusiastic Keighley outfit won 11-7 and Chris and company knew the next eight months was not going to be an easy ride.

A pleasant diversion from Chris's viewpoint was the County Championship, held as usual during September and October. The usual three-way contest between Cumbria, Lancashire and Yorkshire was expanded to include a fourth 'county', labelled 'Other Nationalities', providing players from outside the traditional areas an opportunity to show their mettle ahead of the 1975 World Cup. Chris retained the captaincy of Lancashire but withdrew from the opening match on Wednesday 11 September, a 14-13 win over Other Nationalities at Salford. Chris had played twice for Salford during the previous weekend and aggravated an elbow injury that troubled him since the tour.

Unlike some players – who saw the county matches as a chore – Chris was happy to resume his place in the next fixture seven days later – beating Cumbria 29-4 at Warrington. Another week on and Lancashire travelled to Yorkshire knowing victory would seal the title. Keighley's Lawkholme Lane, though, had suddenly become a bogey ground for Chris, and his team was defeated 20-14, forcing a play-off between the two cross-Pennine rivals. The venue was Naughton Park, Widnes, on Wednesday 16 November, and this time the Red Rose triumphed 29-11, Chris scoring one of Lancashire's five tries, with Ken Gill outstanding on his county debut. The result gave Chris his third County Championship winners' medal. Although he did not realise at the time, it was his last representative game:

> I'm very proud of my three County Championship winners' medals. I've got a couple of Wembley runners-up medals and my World Cup winners' medal for 1972, plus a good few others, but I treasure the ones that I won with Lancashire. I'm not going over the top in saying this, but I played a lot of times for Lancashire – it seemed like a lot anyway – and, being a Wigan lad, I took pride in playing for my county. It probably doesn't mean anything to anybody now, but at the time I thought it was great to be included. To me, it was like taking pride in where you came from. I know that some players were picked and then they soon got fed up of it. After all, it wasn't any big licks going up to Workington on a Tuesday night to play Cumbria, but I always enjoyed the honour of playing for Lancashire.

Meanwhile, Salford's League form was proving erratic. After the Keighley set-back the Reds comfortably overcame Halifax 37-0 at The Willows, but then lost 12-11 to visitors Featherstone Rovers. The next championship fixture, which produced a 24-14 win at York on 15 September, provided a unique experience for Chris. For the only time in his career, and with Eric Prescott being out injured, he started a match at loose forward, packing down in the scrum behind second-row men Dixon and John Knighton.

Chris was back at centre five days later – Gill returning at stand-off for his first match of the season – as Salford won 29-13. One writer claimed 'The good old days were back at Salford last night. For the visit of Dewsbury not only produced the traditional fast, open game – it brought the best out of the champions. And how the fans loved it.' Chris scored two of the tries, one of them through his speciality of following up penalty kick attempts, accepting the rebound off the post to score.

As if to prove the 'good old days' were, indeed, back, the Reds followed up with emphatic home wins over Castleford – 36-5 in the first round of the Players' No.6 Trophy, Chris scoring two more tries – and Keighley, by 45-2. The latter, a League encounter on Wednesday evening, 2 October, in which 'the Yorkshiremen had no answer to the champions speed and class', had a newsworthy sub-plot as Watkins made his reappearance, replacing centre Gordon Graham at half-time. When he took possession of the ball for the first time, Watkins did something unexpected and out of character. Making a break, he ignored his supporting wingman and ran headlong into three Keighley defenders who 'welcomed' him with open arms. 'I wanted to see if I could still take a hammering. I wanted to prove I was totally fit' was his explanation afterwards. Watkins, no doubt satisfied with the outcome, pulled off a bigger surprise the following day when he announced his immediate retirement, the press adding that Chris had succeeded him as skipper:

It's strange, but looking back now, I don't ever remember anybody approaching me and asking me to take over as captain. I was just looking after things at the start of the season and it must have been a case that in the dressing room they said 'Well Watkins is not captain any more, Chris'll be the captain.' Let's put it this way, nobody ever came to me and said 'Chris, we want you to be the new captain'. I think it was just assumed I would do it! I remember that game against Keighley because afterwards I overheard their coach Alan Kellett – who had been a brilliant stand-off with Oldham during the 1950s and 1960s – say to somebody 'That's the best performance I've seen from a team in a long while.' We were certainly on form that night.

Chris's growing celebrity saw him featured as a guest writer for several newspapers and it was during October 1974 that the

Evening Post & Chronicle (the South West Lancashire edition of the *Lancashire Evening Post*) announced his new weekly column in their Saturday *Last Football* sports paper, an arrangement that continued for several years. It was not his first foray into journalism, however, having occasionally written for the paper during 1971, under their 'Guest Spot' section. Also, the Rugby Football League had launched an 'official' weekly paper called *Pro-ball* at the start of 1973 and Chris was invited to offer his opinions under the banner of 'Player's Point of View by Chris Hesketh.' It was also in 1973 that he began airing his thoughts for the *Manchester Evening News* in their Saturday football special edition, under 'Chris Hesketh's Point of View.'

Having played a part in Salford's first two competitive matches of the 1974/75 season, Chris had taken a much-needed ten-day family holiday during August, missing the opening round of the Lancashire Cup, a 25-8 home win over Blackpool Borough. Chris was back in harness to help his team progress through the next two rounds to reach the Final, but was forced to step down from the deciding match with Widnes at Central Park on 2 November. He had been injured when tackled heavily in the 14-8 defeat at Wigan on 19 October and carried from the field on a stretcher. 'I thought I'd broken my leg at first' says Chris, who was later found to have strained the ligaments in his knee and ankle. Despite intensive treatment, leading up to a late fitness check, Chris was to miss a major Final for Salford for the only time in his career. On the morning of the match, Chris told Jack Bentley of the *Daily Express* 'My knee just hasn't improved enough for me to play in a top-class rugby league match. I'm absolutely shattered. People cannot know how disappointed I am.' It was a double blow to Salford, as Gill – just back from injury – was also ruled out with ligament trouble, an injury that sidelined him for a further three months. In a forward dominated match – Salford's Mike Coulman being voted man of the match – the Chemics just won a contest described as an 'old fashioned rugby league game of hard, no-nonsense tackling' by 6-2.

Salford reached their second Final of the season when they defeated Hull Kingston Rovers 27-10 at home on Tuesday 3 December in the semi-final stage of the BBC2 Floodlit Trophy. The competition, as its title implies, was covered by BBC2 who televised the second-half of a tie live each week. Unfortunately, Rovers were delayed getting to Weaste and the match began 35 minutes late, creating a dilemma for the 'Beeb' who had to hastily reschedule, broadcasting the entire match. Although Fielding contributed four tries and three goals it was Peter Banner who stole the show, earning the man of the match award. Banner had been just as valuable to his team in the previous round of the competition three weeks earlier when Salford earned a dramatic 11-7 win over St Helens at Knowsley Road. Jack McNamara had been generous in his praise of the Reds' performance, stating 'Every man tackled bravely, particularly stand-off Chris Hesketh and full-back Paul Charlton.' Chris particularly recalls the match-winner from his scrum-half partner Banner, saying 'He scored a wonderful try, one of his most memorable. He bluffed his way past three defenders who were expecting him to pass wide to Keith Fielding. It was brilliant.'

Salford were favoured by a home draw for the Final against Warrington on Tuesday 17 December, the two teams producing an absorbing match, although it finished scoreless. Once more the BBC were caught on the hop, unexpectedly having to find a slot to accommodate the replay at Wilderspool, eventually arranged for 28 January. A few weeks before the replay took place, Watkins, who had previously said he would help out in an emergency, answered an appeal from Salford coach Les Bettinson. Full-back Charlton was unavailable after fracturing his collarbone and Watkins returned to the side on 10 January, when visitors Wakefield Trinity inflicted a 16-6 defeat on the Reds. Watkins played in the centre whilst Chris, for the only time in a Salford jersey, started the match at full-back. Watkins continued with Salford for over four years before his last match in April 1979, although Chris retained the captaincy.

The conditions for the replayed BBC2 Floodlit Trophy Final could not have been worse. The teams had to endure snow, sleet and rain on a muddy pitch that was hardly conducive to entertaining rugby. As it happened, Salford registered two spectacular first half tries on their way to a 10-5 victory to bring Chris his first trophy as the Reds skipper. The opening try came in the 6th minute when Watkins fielded a long-distance penalty effort from Derek Whitehead to race half the length of the field before sending Fielding sprinting over. Five minutes before the interval the ever-alert Chris intercepted a Barry Philbin pass on the half-way line to send Maurice Richards roaring into the left corner at the railway end for a try that proved decisive and deflated the aspirations of the home fans:

We'd drawn at Salford on a very heavy ground and it was even worse at Wilderspool. It was a very tight match and I remember the team put in a lot of good spadework – if you'll pardon the expression on a pudding of a pitch. The way the conditions were you had to work hard if you were going to win. Our forwards had a big influence on that replay, particularly Alan Grice, Peter Walker and Graham MacKay in the front-row. Alan was never a Cliff Watson or a Dennis Hartley or whoever but, my goodness, he was a great clubman. Graham – a Cumbrian – was another unsung hero. But you need players like Alan and Graham. Some players never reach international level but they'll turn out for you in the middle of the night if you wanted them to. Some of us are lucky to attain representative honours whilst others are, if you like, at a level just underneath. But they're in the game because they love playing rugby. When you think of that front row playing in a cup final that night for Salford, it was like their Wembley really and they deserved every minute of it. It was a magnificent feeling to be carried around the field after we won and it was really good for Salford as a club because it brought them a cup at last, after we had failed to deliver so many times in cup competitions.

McNamara wrote 'What a difference a cup makes! Salford's unexpected Floodlit Trophy Final replay victory in the Wilderspool mud last week silenced their critics and brought an upsurge of interest in the forthcoming Challenge Cup tie at Featherstone.' With Chris receiving high praise from the press for his performance in the replay, McNamara took the opportunity to reflect on what, at times, had been a traumatic season for Salford's leader, writing 'No player has fallen foul of the fans' recent criticism more than skipper Chris Hesketh who was looking lethargic this season after returning from captaining Great Britain on their gruelling tour of Australasia.'

When I came back from the 1974 tour and went straight into another season I was getting comments like 'Get off Hesketh, you're rubbish' and I'd be going up the tunnel to the dressing room after the match and it was around there, really, where people would be shouting at you. To be truthful, I could understand that. It was tough to take but its all part of the game. You take the accolades so you have to take the negatives as well sometimes. I was a yard off the pace to how I normally was. My body was deadly tired without me really knowing it. There were some tired limbs in the Salford team after the 1974 tour. Well, that was certainly true on my part. I'd gone a full season, played in 20 matches on tour and then gone straight back into another season again. I could have done with four weeks' complete rest, but because of injuries, it wasn't possible. I didn't realise – I don't think you do – that you come back feeling as though your fit and everything's fine and you start playing and, all of a sudden you drop the ball or you miss a tackle. I didn't miss a lot of tackles but I always knew when I missed one that I should have made. What I did wrong was to carry on playing, particularly when I had injuries, and I didn't do myself any favours. I suppose whoever is in charge of a team want to put out what they considered to be their best side for every match. I carried on playing and sometimes I could play all right and other times I'd be struggling.

The daunting trip to Featherstone Rovers in the first round of the Challenge Cup on 9 February did not get off to the best start when the team coach broke down on the way. Some players got a lift on a supporters' coach when fans gave up their places. The rest followed in a replacement coach that went the wrong way and arrived with 25 minutes to spare! Salford won the match 17-7, not least because of a huge defensive effort in the opening 20 minutes when Featherstone bombarded the Salford line. Frank Stead – deputising for Charlton – led the way, pulling off some superb tackles on the heavy Rovers forwards, whilst Chris and Jim Fiddler also made great try-line saves. Salford's supporters were so ecstatic, they invaded the Salford dressing room afterwards to congratulate their heroes. The Reds supporters were less delirious two weeks later when bogey team Leeds knocked their team out 17-12 in the second round at The Willows when it was noted that 'too many of Salford's efforts relied on desperate forward barges down the middle.'

McNamara was at his poetic best in trying to make sense of the Reds' yo-yo season. He wrote: 'Following Salford devotedly must be like courting a delightful but fickle woman. The moments of fulfilment are marvellous, but the disappointments are bitterly frustrating. Salford are struggling with a distinct grating noise coming from the usual smooth-running attacking machine and a defence that has been made to look dubious too often for comfort. "The crowd is getting at us and it doesn't help" says skipper Chris Hesketh. "I had a go at somebody in the crowd during the

Wakefield match because he was getting at (recent signing) Jim Fiddler. He really was going at him so when I went to retrieve the ball from touch I told him to shut up and give the lad a chance. There are only a few in the crowd like this, but they make their presence felt."' 'I do remember doing that' says Chris, 'and I think I used a few choice words as well! It was something I regretted afterwards. It's not my style to do something like that but it was sheer frustration.'

Chris continued to be a target and after the Easter Monday clash with Wigan on 31 March, Bettinson went into print to defend his captain. 'They lined up to boo him – it was disgusting' he said, 'The attitude of the supporters has never been so bad. The coach is always held accountable and I accept this. Hesketh's form has slipped but he's played his heart out for years.' The reason for the supporters' ire was that Salford's 20-30 defeat, which followed the Good Friday 18-9 loss at Rochdale Hornets, had seen the team slide dangerously close to the relegation zone. Chris, who was not the only focus of disapproval, had, in fact, played against Wigan with a bad dose of influenza, which caused him to miss the next two games.

Salford, finished in ninth place in the League and gained a credible 20-12 away win at Challenge Cup finalists Widnes in the first round of the Premiership Trophy on Sunday 27 April, only to be eliminated two days later at Wigan 35-17. The Reds had one further commitment, flying out to Marseille the next day to play the French national side, part of a Festival of Sport organised in the town:

The French side were preparing for the 1975 World Cup. We lost 23-13 but that wasn't bad when you think we had just finished a long season and had only played at Wigan the night before. We were also short of several first team players that were unable to make the trip. The match took place in the Stade Velodrome, a magnificent stadium where they also played international matches. Marseille is a beautiful place and there was a harbour only a few hundred yards away from out hotel. In the evening Charlo and myself went to this bar and we had a bottle or two each, although Charlo wasn't a big drinker. All of a sudden these blokes came in. They looked like real 'heavies' and we were thinking 'Whoops! This doesn't look too good.' We were listening to them jabbering away to one another in French and just as we were thinking 'We'd better get out of here just to be on the safe side' Mike Coulman and Jim Fiddler – both big forwards – and one or two others walked in, so we said 'Oh, we're all right now, we'll have another!' We flew over to France in a private jet that belonged to the French Rugby League president, which was incredible. It was also a nice change for a lot of the players in our team who played their rugby week-in week-out in England and never went to places like Australia, New Zealand or France. It was only a few days but it was great. That was typical of the style of Salford under Brian Snape. It was just a bit different.

With the summer break behind him, Chris was in better shape to face the rigours of the 1975/76 season compared to 12 months ago. One story that emerged as the season opened was how badly he had been affected through injury in the previous campaign, in particular through a nagging back injury, which Chris admitted had affected his form. 'I was suffering from fluid on the nerve in my back. It was affecting my right leg and I was worried about it, but I couldn't rest it. I've been having manipulative treatment and hope to be right for the start of the season' he said at the time.

Salford broke the bank again, paying out a new rugby league record £15,000 for Featherstone Rovers scrum-half Steve Nash during August 1975. 'Stevie Nash was a brilliant world class scrum-half' says Chris, 'He was like an extra forward on the field and wasn't scared of going in and mixing it. He was always willing to take the ball and give the forwards a rest for a minute.' It was Nash who later gave an insight into Chris's exuberant dressing room personality, when he said, in a *Manchester Evening News* football edition in December 1977: 'He is still one of the best centres in the game. He is also one of the funniest men off the field and never stops talking. The lads recently had Chris a bet after training to see if he could keep quiet for five minutes and he was the most surprised of all when he won.'

Salford, in contrast to the previous season, got off to a much livelier start, and were not beaten in the League until mid-December. All the old superlatives were being banded about in the press with references to 'vintage rugby' and 'class and speed.' Tom Bergin in the *Salford City Reporter* was particularly taken by Salford's 30-10 win over Widnes at The Willows on 5 September, saying to his readers: 'Many of you over the years must have wearied of my references to the old (1930s) Red Devils. On Friday, the 1975 Reds were on a par with their illustrious predecessors.' Bergin also gave praise to 'a captains display from Chris Hesketh.'

Chris, himself, was in sparkling form, rediscovering his brilliant best to once more become one of Salford's 'favourite sons' as far as the Reds' supporters were concerned. In the 37-10 win at Oldham on 16 November, the second of Chris's two tries was his one hundredth for the club. Twelve days later, Salford won a vital home match against Featherstone Rovers 13-7 to go joint top of the Division One table with Widnes. The Reds had trailed 4-2 until just before half-time, when Chris, sidestepping from a scrum 35 yards out, wrong-footed Rovers' full-back Harold Box to sprint between the posts. It gave his team a vital, psychological 7-4 interval lead over a side that had also started the season well, giving them the confidence to go out and complete the job in the second half.

Whilst Salford displayed good League form, their cup results, as usual, were a bit mixed. In an era when clubs had five knock-out events to aim at, they had a spell, during September and October, of playing six consecutive ties across three different competitions. They suffered an early dismissal in defence of the BBC2 Floodlit Trophy – losing 25-19 at Wigan in a replay – but reached the Lancashire Cup Final, for the fourth successive year, in style. After outclassing Huyton at home by 44-17, they had faced a potential 'banana skin' when travelling to Leigh for the second round. Salford won 23-6 but their hosts gave the Reds a tough match. 'We knew it was going to be hard' said Chris afterwards, 'but it was a matter of not making mistakes and waiting for our chances – and we proved we can be patient.'

They faced an even sterner challenge in the semi-final when they were drawn away to St Helens on the evening of Tuesday 23 September. After going 5-0 behind, Salford put on a blistering show of attacking rugby. At 5-3, Chris started the move that led to the go-ahead try, sucking in winger Les Jones before providing the alert Richards with an inside pass, the Welshman evading Billy Benyon and rounding Geoff Pimblett for a converted try that put the Red Devils 8-5 up. A rampant Salford extended their lead to 15-5 by half-time eventually earning their place in the Final with a 21-8 scoreline.

The Final was a repeat of the previous year, Salford facing Widnes at Central Park on Saturday 4 October. Chris was in optimistic mood prior to the match saying 'If we can show the teamwork and the team spirit of the last few weeks we should do well. I'm confident but I'm not daft. Widnes are a good, hardworking team, but if we get our share of luck we'll win.' Unfortunately for Salford, the luck did go against them to a degree, the match being played in driving rain on a muddy pitch:

I suppose for the spectators it was a dour match and wasn't a classic game at all. The heavy conditions were much more suited to the heavier Widnes pack and, also, we were well beaten for scrum possession and played without the ball for long periods. It was another example, I suppose, that for all the good teams we had at Salford during those years, we never really got the pack right and that often cost us in the big cup matches. To be fair to Widnes, they were well worth their 16-7 win. The semi-final at St Helens was a much happier occasion from the Salford point of view – it's just a pity it wasn't the Final! To me as a Wiganer, it was always a big game going to Knowsley Road and we really went well that night.

Further examples of the inability to stand up to their opposition when the stakes are high reared its ugly head in the Players' No.6 Trophy and the Rugby League Challenge Cup. They reached the semi-final stage of the former with comparative ease and were favoured to progress to the Final after receiving a home draw to Division Two side Hull. Broadcast live by the BBC on Saturday 13 December, Salford was unable to hold an efficient, ruthless Hull pack and lost 22-14. There were repercussions when Bettinson substituted forwards Prescott and Fiddler at half-time – when Hull had built up a 15-4 lead – Chris moving to loose-forward for the last 40 minutes. The pair – clearly aggrieved – refused to sit on the bench after the interval and returned to the dressing room, leaving Salford without substitutes for the remainder of the match. As skipper, Chris said at the time: 'No player is bigger than the club. It's a sad day for Salford when something like this happens.' The two vowed not to play for Salford again and, although Fiddler never did, the rift with Prescott was quickly patched up.

In the Challenge Cup, Salford raised hopes by convincingly trouncing Castleford 25-3 in the first round at Wheldon Road. Having already won at St Helens in the Lancashire Cup, there were grounds for optimism when the Saints visited The Willows in the second round. Only a few months earlier Chris – his enthusiasm rekindled and feeling more like his old self after the rigours of the previous season – confessed to one journalist 'Before I retire I want to hold the Challenge Cup aloft at Wembley.' But he was to be denied yet again when, on Sunday 29 February, watched by over 13,000, the day ended with another cup flop as the Reds lost 17-11. McNamara was in no doubt about where he thought the problem lay, saying 'Until they achieve that long-sought blend of power and speed in the pack, they are going to fail in more cup competitions – and no discredit to the six forwards who worked so hard against the Saints.'

> I really wouldn't want to say this as derogatory to any of the Salford lads, particularly the forwards, but I think we had the backs but were just short with the pack. We could go to places like Featherstone as the so-called 'crème de la crème' and their pack would take a grip on the game and get ten points on the board and that was it. Some of the doubters called us the 'Quality Street Gang' and we deserved it – because we were quality! When we went to Yorkshire though, everybody over there used to give us stick over that name, calling us the 'soft centres'. But we were a very, very, good side. Sadly – and I don't know the reason for it – but we never quite got the forwards right. We had some good grafters in the forwards but we could have been better again with a more damaging pack. But the main thing was that, as players, we loved it. We always tried to be entertainers and I think the fans enjoyed it too, except for the cup defeats, obviously. I remember Cliff Evans used to say to us 'Look, go out and enjoy it, you've got pace to burn, run them all over the field' and, more often than not, we did.

Meanwhile, having won their opening nine League fixtures, Salford had suffered a mid-season wobble and, from the next six Division One matches, only one – at home to Bradford Northern on 28 December – produced a victory. The 20-10 win over Northern saw Chris, who transferred to loose-forward again during the game, in outstanding form, as he 'scored an excellent try and worked tirelessly on attack and in defence to take the man of the match award.' According to press reports it earned him a set of car tyres from sponsor, National Tyre Service, but a bemused Chris has no recollection of that happening, joking 'You'd think I'd remember taking four tyres home wouldn't you?'

Salford revitalised their Championship bid with an unexpected 13-4 win at Wakefield Trinity on 25 January on the back of three well-taken tries including one from Chris. The result not only avenged a home defeat by Trinity a month earlier, but knocked their Yorkshire rivals off the top of the table. Chris grabbed two further tries in the next match, a 36-30 home win over Wigan on 3 February, recovering from an early 10-3 deficit with Chris, as he so often did against his former club, having 'a particularly strong match in the centre.' With 12 Division One fixtures remaining it left Salford – who had the better scoring record – level on points with Featherstone Rovers at the head of the table, with Wakefield Trinity one point behind. Whilst Trinity fell away in the dying months, Featherstone and Salford stayed neck-and-neck with Leeds coming up on the rails as the vital Easter fixtures approached.

The weekend before Easter, Salford despatched visitors Huddersfield 24-9 on Friday 9 April, but suffered a huge blow to their title aspirations during the match when Chris damaged his ligaments when he twisted his knee, making him unavailable for the Easter holiday games. Also of concern to the Salford cause was the absence of Gill, who stayed away for the remainder of the season after being dropped to substitute for the 19-3 home win over Hull Kingston Rovers on 2 April.

Despite the loss of their captain, Salford won both Easter fixtures; 30-22 at Swinton on Good Friday, and 24-15 at Wigan on Easter Monday. With one game left, Salford led the table by a single point from Featherstone Rovers, but the odds favoured Rovers, who had a match in hand on the Reds. Leeds were also nicely positioned to pounce, three points behind Salford but with three matches remaining. Bettinson conceded that the situation did not look promising for Salford, saying 'I don't think we'll win it. I fancy Featherstone for the title. They've got two home matches to go and I can't see them slipping up now.'

In a dramatic and unexpected finish, matching that of Salford's Championship success two years earlier, the picture changed in the Reds' favour. Firstly, a nervous-looking Featherstone Rovers suffered a shock home defeat to Hull Kingston Rovers by 17-9 on Wednesday 21 April and then, two days later, Wigan inflicted a crucial – from Salford's point of view – 27-15 win over Leeds at Central Park. It left Salford in the position of travelling to Keighley the following Sunday for the last match knowing victory would bring the Division One Championship back to The Willows for the second time in three seasons.

Chris returned to the team for the trip to Lawkholme Lane, which, on paper, looked certain to provide Salford with the two points needed. Keighley were third-bottom in the table with relegation assured. Chris, though, was not so sure, saying at the time 'I'm decidedly uneasy, I've been to Keighley before and lost. But, having said that, everyone seems to be playing well at the moment, particularly the forwards. They have performed wonders in our last two matches. I hope thousands come with us, because they can lift the team. Barring accidents, we should be Champions, which will be nice for a lot of people – and not only the players.' Although Salford only won 18-10, they made virtually certain with a three-try salvo in the opening 18 minutes of the match to lead 11-0. McNamara commented 'Hesketh, although he was not 100 per cent fit after injury, handled the team well under some very tough Keighley pressure.' Chris, transformed from villain to hero in 12 months, was triumphantly chaired around the field by the excited Salford fans after the match. He said 'I'm delighted for the chairman's sake and for our supporters as much as for the players. We worked hard for the title and we made it.'

I shouldn't have played that day because of my knee ligament problem. It was my left knee, which was – and still is – my worst knee, and there is no way I should have been on that field even though it was such an important game. I think it was a case of 'strap him up and get him out there!' and I suppose from one point of view with 80 minutes to get through to win the Championship, I could do it. Our half-backs Steve Nash and John Butler played well that day and we got off to a quick start. When Mike Coulman went charging through for our third try early on, I thought we'd won it. But then I suppose nerves set in. Then Colin Dixon raced in from about 30 yards out to get that vital second half try, and it was a big relief. It was a nice moment afterwards when I was carried around the field by the fans. So we won the Championship for the second tine in three years – that wasn't bad was it?

Four weeks later, at Swinton on Saturday 22 May, Salford appeared in their only Premiership Trophy Final, a contest introduced the previous season to replace the short-lived and cumbersome Club Merit Championship. Salford reached the decider against St Helens after trouncing Hull Kingston Rovers 21-6 in the first round at The Willows, and then beating Wakefield Trinity in a two-legged semi-final. Having only lost 10-5 in the first leg, Trinity approached the return on their Belle Vue ground with confidence. It was a confidence quickly shattered by a neat Watkins drop-goal after only eight minute, which pushed Trinity two scores behind. The Red Devils went on to grab two tries before they 'crowned their victory three minutes from the end when Richards broke way to gain the position from which Dixon sent skipper Chris Hesketh darting and dodging between the Trinity posts.' The Final was a clash of Champions versus Challenge Cup winners, St Helens having beaten Widnes at Wembley two weeks earlier. Salford, although they had some early chances, never reproduced their best form in a match that was dominated by the forwards, Saints scoring three tries in the last 12 minutes to win 15-2.

Although the result provided a disappointing end to the campaign, it could not remove the gloss from what, on the whole, had been an excellent campaign for players and supporters. Bettinson was lavish in his praise of Chris's contribution to the cause, saying 'He's Mr Rugby League. He is one of the finest players I have known because of his dedication and completely professional approach. He is an outstanding captain. His influence is first-class on the field, off the field, and in the dressing room. As well as being a good footballer, he's an iron man physically.'

10

A GENTLEMANLY FIGURE

The Queen's New Years Honours List in January 1976, included the name 'Chris Hesketh MBE', the *Evening Post & Chronicle* declaring his recognition 'A tribute to one of the most gentlemanly figures the game has known' adding that 'it also carries a message of hope to all polio victims.' Chris was only the fourth rugby league player honoured, following the awarding of MBEs to his former Wigan coach Eric Ashton in 1966, Hunslet stalwart Geoff Gunney in 1970, and World Cup winning captain Clive Sullivan in 1974:

A letter came to our house and on it, it said 'On Her Majesty's Service' or something like that. I opened it up and it was a letter from the Prime Minister, Harold Wilson, telling me of my nomination. It said 'Sir, the Queen has it in mind etc, etc.' 'What's all this?' I thought to myself. I read it again and said 'Hey, look at this from my sister' because it arrived quite close to my birthday in November and I thought my sister was having a joke with me. I thought it was one of them daft letters you send to people. But it wasn't of course. When the day came to receive my award, it was brilliant because my mam went with me to Buckingham Palace. And it was a good day out – let's put it that way! One company I worked for wanted to include it on my business card – 'Chris Hesketh MBE' – but I said 'No'. To me it sounds like you're boasting. Of course, it's good personally to receive it, but I also felt that the Salford club and rugby league in general had been honoured. As far as I'm concerned, though, it doesn't change your life at all.

Apart from being presented to the Queen for my award, when she said a few words of congratulation to me, I met Her Majesty a second time – although it was just a handshake on that occasion! It was on Thursday 9 July 1992 at a garden party in the grounds of Buckingham Palace. It was for people who had achieved a lot in sport during Her Majesty's 40-year reign, as it was then. Obviously, there were a lot of sporting celebrities present. I particularly remember seeing members of England's 1966 World Cup winning side and several boxers such as Henry Cooper and Chris Eubank.

So, 'Chris Hesketh MBE' led his troops into the 1976/77 season intent on retaining the Championship, although the main priority was that elusive return to Wembley Stadium. The first blow was losing 14-13 at Warrington on 29 August in the second round of the Lancashire Cup, thus breaking the sequence of consecutive Final appearances, which stood at four – a club record. A few days later, on 3 September, Salford gained revenge over Warrington in their opening match of the Division One campaign, winning 16-5 at The Willows, Jack McNamara commenting in the *Manchester Evening News* that 'Chris Hesketh played well, both in the centre and then at loose forward after (John) Mantle retired.'

During the first half of the season, it appeared as though Salford's grip on the Championship trophy was loosening, winning just six and drawing one of their opening 14 fixtures prior to the turn of the year. Chris, although moving into 'veteran' status as a player, was still providing touches of magic. In the 16-16 home draw with Hull Kingston Rovers on 24 September, he bamboozled three defenders in scoring a try that brought the Reds back into contention when they were behind, whilst in the 33-6 win over Rochdale Hornets – also at home – on 8 October, McNamara remarked on the 'spectacular solo try by captain Chris Hesketh from inside his own half.' Coach Les Bettinson, commenting on the latter match, said 'It was a step forward (for the team) and some of the older men proved they can still run a bit – Hesketh turned back the clock five years.'

Chris was unable to turn out at all during November, when it was admitted that he had been playing with the aid of pain-killing tablets because of a damaged back. 'I'm not looking for sympathy' said Chris at the time, 'It's my fault that I've carried on playing. I've got a trapped nerve in the back of my neck and get referral pain in my right shoulder down my arm to my thumb. I have suffered from this for 14 or 15 months. It is very sore the day after a match, but gradually improves over the week before the next match – and it is surprising what a couple of painkillers can do!' He was also advised to wear a surgical collar, something he had done several times in the previous year. Chris, who was becoming more and more battle scarred, also needed an operation on his nose. 'It's been broken four times and I can't breathe through one nostril' he admitted, 'I've been told by a specialist that it needs surgery quickly because infection could set in. I'm in a quandary about the matter.' Bettinson showed concern, saying 'A normal man would have been off work with such an injury, but Chris is an iron man. He drives himself harder than anyone.'

Injuries are an occupational hazard in rugby league. Kenny Gill would say to me 'Just run into that gap and I'll put the ball there.' And the joke is; yes, I did score quite a lot of tries off that move, but I also got a bloody bad nose! It got to the stage with my nose where I could break it and not really bother about it because they'd say there's nothing there. I went to see this specialist and he said 'We can fix your nose for you. We'll take a bit of bone off your hip.' I said 'Hang on just a minute, what do you mean a bit of bone?' Then he said 'How long are you thinking of carrying on playing?' and I replied 'I don't know – maybe two or three years.' 'Well you're better off not having it done until you stop playing' so

I never had it done!

Chris returned to action in December, despite an x-ray revealing that his neck and back trouble was due to a shortened disc. 'It's painful but not serious. There's no treatment and I shall just have to put up with it' said Chris at the time. Salford's 1977 Challenge Cup campaign was due to get under way in mid-February against Huddersfield, the Reds raising their fans hopes once again by hitting peak form in winning the four preceding fixtures as they climbed up the Division One table. The last of those wins was the biggest upset of all. Salford travelled to Headingley on Saturday 5 February, registering their first away win over Leeds since 1959, ending a run of 12 consecutive defeats. 'We won 28-13 and, for once, we hammered them at Headingley' recalls Chris, 'We scored six tries and I remember that I got one of them. Leeds were winning 10-0 at one point but we got it back to 10-10 by half-time. But it was the only time we won there!' That unexpected success brought Salford up to second place in the League table, two points behind St Helens.

The following Friday, Salford won their first round Challenge Cup tie over Huddersfield by a cosy 25-2 at The Willows. Gill withdrew just before kick-off with a heavy cold, Chris partnering Steve Nash at half-back, the pair having a big influence on what was a good team performance. Two weeks later, on 27 February, Salford travelled to Workington Town for the second round. Chris predicted 'It's going to be blooming hard. They always play harder against us than anybody else.' Unfortunately for Salford, his words rang true, losing 13-4 in a match dominated by the defences and described by the *Manchester Evening News* as 'typical cup-tie rugby.' Salford – who managed just two penalties off the boot of David Watkins – had their best try-scoring opportunity in the 56th minute when Chris made a powerful break before passing to Nash ten yards from the Workington posts. A certain score was thwarted, though, when winger John Risman appeared from nowhere to make a critical tackle. A week later there was more despair for Salford fans when their team lost a crucial 'four-pointer' League match at St Helens by 29-9. Afterwards, Bettinson provided his own shock by deciding it was time to step down as coach. Colin Dixon, who claimed he was 'stunned' to be asked, took over as player–coach.

After the St Helens loss, Salford dropped out of Championship contention and eventually finished sixth. The last League fixture was at home to Leeds on Sunday 24 April, and it was to end tragically. The visitors' 23-year-old stand-off, Chris Sanderson, reportedly injured whilst making a tackle in the 8th minute of the game and subsequently taken off on a stretcher before being rushed to Hope Hospital, died there shortly after his arrival:

> I vaguely remember there was a melee of players and when it broke up he was on the ground. When he was being carried off I didn't really know who it was at the time. Just before half-time Syd Hynes, who was managing Leeds then, came onto the halfway line and shouted to me 'Chris, you'll have to stop the match.' In the confusion, I'm not sure if he said to me 'Chris Sanderson was dead', but I think he did. Syd had presumably heard from the hospital – thinking about it now he must have – and I ran to the referee, Bill Allen, and said to him 'You'd better blow your whistle.' I can't remember the exact words I used but I told him that the lad had died. And then they announced it over the loudspeaker and it was just terrible. Nobody really spoke in the dressing room afterwards. Most of us went to his funeral in York and, as you can imagine, that was a very sad occasion. You see a lot of things happen on a rugby field and it's a tough place to be for anybody but, for all that the game can be like at times, you never expect that.

The match – with Leeds winning 5-2 – was abandoned after 38

minutes and declared void. A week later, Salford's first trophy-less season, after four consecutive campaigns of collecting silverware, came to an end when they lost 25-17 at Castleford in the first round of the Premiership Trophy. According to one report 'no one did more to try and keep Salford on the right path than Chris Hesketh in attack and Gordon Graham in defence', Chris scoring the second of his sides three tries.

It was not the most auspicious of openings to a season for Chris in 1977/78, failing to complete either of Salford's pre-season friendly games. He retired after 28 minutes with slight concussion in the 23-15 win at Leigh on 9 August, and lasted 56 minutes at Swinton five days later through a back injury, a match the Reds won 35-15. Chris then set off for a two-week family holiday in Bournemouth, no doubt hoping to recuperate, but – due to an early-season injury crisis – Salford planned to interrupt his break by flying him back for the Lancashire Cup tie at Workington on 21 August. The idea was eventually shelved as Chris had not fully recovered from his back injury.

Salford started the League campaign well, winning seven of the first eight matches, and led the table during October. They came unstuck, though, in their next two Division One fixtures; losing 14-7 at Wakefield – minus Chris who was suffering from bruised ribs – on 13 November, and at St Helens, 13-12 on 27 November. Sports writer Alan Thomas, commenting on the latter match, wrote 'Salford produced staying power which I didn't think they possessed. Inside 12 minutes, Saints had romped to a 10-0 lead. Salford produced their own brand of high speed rugby with Chris Hesketh showing flashes of the form which made him the games best centre three years ago.' Nine days later, Salford were back at Knowsley Road to face Saints in the semi-final of the BBC2 Floodlit Trophy – only the second time the Reds had got to that stage of the competition – but lost a tight match 7-4.

At the beginning of January, Dixon – Salford having won only two of their previous nine matches – resigned as player–coach, citing 'pressure of business' after recently taking over a public house. Chris agreed to take charge of the team on a temporary basis until a successor was found. 'I have agreed to look after things for the time being' said Chris, whilst urging the club to appoint a new coach as a matter of priority. 'We need it for cohesion and for the sake of the players' state of mind' he said at the time.

By the end of January, Salford surprised the rugby league community with the announcement of 54-year-old Stan McCormick as the new coach. A star winger in the 1940s and 1950s for Belle Vue Rangers, St Helens and Warrington, he had not been involved in the sport since quitting as St Helens coach in 1965. Reportedly, Salford had tried and failed to recruit Ray French, the former St Helens and Widnes forward, destined to talk to a wider audience when replacing Eddie Waring as BBC Television's rugby league commentator in the 1981/82 season.

Chris actually had charge of team affairs from 6 January until 28 January, a period that covered five matches, the first two of which were won. Out injured with knee ligament trouble and severe neck pain at the time, he was unable to take part in any of them. McCormick – given the job until the end of the season – was dismissed after only seven weeks and four matches, the last one being a second round Challenge Cup exit at Huddersfield on 12 March by 13-3. This time, team trainer Alan McInnes was asked to be caretaker coach until the end of the season, the fourth man in charge in under three months:

Personally, I was surprised when Colin Dixon took over as coach in the first place. It wasn't because I thought Colin wouldn't make a good coach. He was a brilliant player as we know and a cracking bloke to be with but he hadn't got any coaching experience at that time. You need certain qualities to coach a team at the top level and that's the same for anybody. To throw him into being coach of a professional team was asking a lot. To be honest, Colin was as shocked as anybody at the time. He didn't hold his hand up for the Salford job, although I know he wanted to get involved in coaching after he stopped playing.

Salford did the same with me really because I wanted to concentrate on playing. As far as the coaching job was concerned I just said 'Okay, I'll help you out, but I don't want it permanently.' I suppose as a senior professional at the club I felt a sense of duty. Whilst I was in charge, there was one match at Featherstone when we got hammered 40-8. I remember that I was sat there on the touchline thinking 'What the so-and-so's going on here?' They were knocking on, they were missing tackles, and it was awful to sit through because I felt helpless. You can do all the talking you want in the dressing room, but once they're out there it's down to them. When you're on the field with them you can cover things a bit – you can't cover things from the dugout can you? To be honest it wasn't something I enjoyed and I was glad to hand it over.

Taking on Stan McCormick wasn't a good move on Salford's part really because I think he'd probably been out of the game too long. To be fair, I would be doing the man a disservice by giving an opinion on him as Salford coach because I don't remember that much about it, because he was only there a short time. I think, when Alan McInnes took over, it steadied things a bit until the end of the season. Alan did a good job in a difficult situation. You could tell he knew what training people was all about, it was second nature to him.

Although Salford again finished sixth in the Division One table, their form -particularly in the second half of the season – had been abysmal at times, and comments about the team's displays such as 'listless and half-hearted' and 'out thought and out tackled' were becoming more frequent. Chris, at 33 years old, was permanently struggling with injuries and missed 10 of the last 18 matches, although – through good times and bad – he still earned plaudits from the press when he did manage to turn out. In a 21-3 home win over Leeds on 3 February – an encouraging result in what was McCormick's first match in charge – it was noted that 'The return of Chris Hesketh tightened up the defence.' Three weeks later, as Salford showed another side of their character in just managing to squeeze past Bramley 9-7 in a first round Challenge Cup tie at The Willows, it was stated 'Salford captain Chris Hesketh worked hard to rally his flagging team.'

Salford's last chance of silverware disappeared when they lost 29-11 at St Helens in the first round of the Premiership Trophy on 30 April although, for most of the Salford squad, there was one more match still to play. On Sunday 21 May 1978, at Cwmbran in South Wales, Chris captained a Salford XIII against a Watkins-led Welsh XIII, in a special challenge match organised as part of their joint-testimonial. Chris's team, which won 40-39, included Paul Charlton – who had returned to Workington Town in 1975 – and Hull Kingston Rovers' Roger Millward.

A testimonial for two of the Red Devils' most famous players – who both completed ten years service with the club during 1977 – was first mooted in the press during September 1976 when it was announced 'Plans are now being discussed at Salford for a bumper joint-benefit for David Watkins and skipper Chris Hesketh.' It was officially launched at the club's Willows Variety Centre with a champagne buffet during December 1977. Attended by businessmen and personalities from both codes of rugby as well as soccer, the two took turns to address the gathering, thanking the organisers and referring to their happy times in rugby league. It was stated 'Many fund-raising events are planned for these two popular footballers' and one writer said 'It seems likely the benefit will be a record in the League.' It was an accurate prediction, the illustrious pair eventually receiving record testimonial cheques of £6,300 each in February 1979, on an evening that saw the launch of another joint-benefit, for forwards Mike Coulman and Colin Dixon.

The 1978/79 season promised to be almost as eventful off the field as on it, after the announcement in May 1978 that Alex Murphy – who had already achieved considerable success in charge of Leigh and Warrington – would be the new coach. Whilst no one could question Murphy's excellent credentials, some concerns were expressed as to whether his abrasive manner would gel with the club's senior professionals. At the press conference to officially announce his appointment, Murphy said 'Salford are no longer to be known as the Quality Street Gang. I can see next season being a good one for us, and I would not be surprised if we went back to Wembley.'

One of the first decisions made by Murphy was to appoint Steve Nash as the team captain with Chris being made vice-captain. It was difficult to argue with Murphy's reasoning, when he explained 'I'm looking to the future and to a lad who can captain the club for a number of years. I greatly admire Hesketh as a dedicated professional and have explained my views to him. Nash, like Hesketh, is an inspiration to the team.'

> You couldn't fault his record as a coach and he's the best scrum-half I've ever seen but he had his own way of running a team. But he also coached Lancashire and England, so people obviously thought he was capable of coaching at county and country level. But, unfortunately, you can't always do it just by being the best player yourself over the last 20 years. You've got to have that ability to deal with the players, as well as being able to motivate them and lead them. It didn't quite work out for him at Salford, although I know he did stay at the club for two and a half years. There were one or two personality clashes, but I have to say I didn't fall out with him at all. In actual fact, in some of the newspapers he said one or two very complimentary things

about me.

I wasn't close friends with Murphy but we certainly weren't enemies. On one occasion during the season we went together to Fylde Rugby Union Club to watch a player. I can't remember now who we went to see, although I'm pretty sure it wasn't David Stephenson, the centre that they signed from Fylde in December 1978. I didn't often go scouting and I think the only other time was when I went up to Northumberland with Cliff Evans in November 1974. The match was at the County Ground in Gosforth and Northumberland were playing Lancashire. There were rumours that we had gone to watch Lancashire forward Fran Cotton, who played for Coventry at the time, but it was actually another England international, Roger Uttley, who was the Northumberland captain. But, in the end, they didn't sign him.

Although he was still, occasionally, used in the centre, Chris played the majority of his matches at stand-off during 1978/79, usually partnering Nash. He continued to struggle through the pain barrier with his various injuries, but, commendably, missed only ten matches all season.

Salford got off to a good start under their new coach, winning their first four matches and reaching the semi-finals of the Lancashire Cup when they entertained Workington Town on 13 September, only to lose 9-8 in a fierce contest in which Chris had to quit with concussion. When Workington returned for the League encounter on 27 October, Salford's defence was more fragile and they were jeered and slow-handclapped off the field at half-time by their own fans, the score standing at 13-0 for Town. Workington eventually won 24-8, McNamara commenting 'The only hint of resistance came when Chris Hesketh appeared midway through the second half as substitute. Hesketh went to stand-off and immediately gingered up the attack.'

Chris started in 25 matches during the campaign although, in truth, he struggled to remain on the field for the full 80 minutes in many of them due to his catalogue of injuries. Knee ligament problems saw him limp off the field after just 18 minutes against Bradford Northern on 29 September, and after 52 minutes at Castleford on 24 November. He fared better, however, in the Boxing Day clash with Widnes, McNamara saying 'Three Salford veterans – Colin Dixon, Mike Coulman and Chris Hesketh – showed that experience and enthusiasm can compensate for the loss of youthful dash in yesterday's thrilling 10-10 draw against Widnes at The Willows' adding 'Stand-off Hesketh fought a great duel with the sturdy Mick Burke.'

Generally, though, Salford was having a very depressing season. Following home defeats by Rochdale Hornets on 23 January, and Leigh on 2 February, Murphy had a 45-minute 'showdown' meeting with the players who, reportedly, were unhappy at playing under him and upset about his shouting comments from the bench. Afterwards, Murphy announced he had the full support of the players.

But Salford's poor run continued and they reached a new low in being knocked out of the Rugby League Challenge Cup in the first round by Division Two mid-table side Bramley. Played on 1 March at Swinton, the 'Villagers' – having held the Reds in two drawn matches already – won 7-5 in a second replay. Disgruntled Salford fans voted with their feet and only 2,743 turned out for their attractive looking home fixture with Leeds eight days later. In an improved performance Salford lost 3-0 with Chris being skipper in the absence of Nash, Jack Bentley, in the *Daily Express*, commenting 'stand-off Chris Hesketh set the pattern with some magnificent early tackles and the response from his colleagues was excellent.'

After the team had been announced for the first Challenge Cup meeting with Bramley, at The Willows on Sunday 11 February, the press made a big play out of the fact that Chris had been relegated to the substitutes bench by Murphy following the team's recent poor form, one report saying 'One of the illustrious heads that rolled in Salford's seven changes was that of centre Chris Hesketh, dropped for the first time in 12 years.' Murphy was quoted as saying 'I made the changes because I have been bitterly disappointed by recent displays, but Chris Hesketh still figures in my plans.' Chris said at the time 'It hurts and I don't think I was the only one to blame. But things have been going badly and I appreciate changes had got to be made. But I'm not falling out with anybody, and there's no panic about my future career.' Chris had been on the Salford bench several times in the past but – with the exception of one match in 1967 – it had occurred when he was returning from absence:

I have total respect for Murphy making that decision. I'm sure I was disappointed at the time – you always want to be in the team – but I was at the back end of my career and they had to try and bring in the younger players. I think it was made a fuss of in the press because it was unusual for me not to be picked. For most of my time at Salford I was never dropped, and probably was never likely to be. I was always in the team and I think eventually it got to the stage where, suddenly, they were saying 'Where's Hesketh?' I think that's all it was.

At the beginning of March, and with the team hovering above the relegation places in the League, there were further reports of player unrest. One player, reportedly, stated the team was unhappy about public criticism from Murphy. Another meeting was arranged, this time with members of the board present:

That meeting took place in the Willows Variety Centre. Whoever was organising it from the players' point of view I don't know but it certainly wasn't me. What they were aiming for was to get Murphy out, but, in the end, it didn't work. There were a lot of seasoned professionals at Salford and they weren't prepared to listen to Murphy standing there reading them the riot act. They asked me to sign a 'round robin' – a petition in other words – but I said 'I don't sign round robins.' I'd never signed a round robin in my life. I would never do something like that.

As the team struggled towards the end of the season, eventually finishing 12th – one place above relegation and their poorest showing for years – Chris received praise from Murphy. The Salford coach publicly expressed his gratitude when Chris played in a home match with Wakefield Trinity during March when he 'volunteered to play although he was unfit with a painful and long-standing neck injury.' For another match, at Rochdale Hornets, Chris again turned out when Salford had 18 players unavailable through injury. 'He's doing a wonderful job for the club. I don't know how he keeps playing with this injury, yet he had a fine match at stand-off' was Murphy's comment.

Having missed the 12-5 defeat at Warrington on 2 May – due to his neck problem – Chris returned for the club's final two matches of the season. It was a tough-looking weekend schedule, Salford winning 26-13 at Wigan on Saturday 12 May – his last appearance at Central Park – followed by a 26-4 defeat at St Helens the next day. The latter – in which Chris had to quit at half-time through his recurring neck problem – was to be his last competitive match.

He did make one more appearance at the tail-end of the season, on Sunday 20 May 1979, when Salford beat Swinton 27-20 in a light-hearted match played at The Willows as part of the Coulman–Dixon Testimonial. A diversion came when Granada Television did some filming for their drama series 'Fallen Hero.' Its star, Del Henney – who played Gareth Hopkins, a rugby league player eventually forced out of the game through injury – and the players provided the camera crew with 'action' shots during the half-time break.

With Watkins having retired during April, former Salford rugby league legend Gus Risman said of him and Chris: 'They have fitted in with all the players they have ever played with, whether it be Great Britain, England, Wales and most of all, Salford. Salford have been lucky to have been able to parade these two Peter Pan players in front of The Willows crowd for so long.'

11

I'M NOT GOING AGAIN!

Chris did not rush his decision to retire after the 1978/79 season, not fully realising himself that the match at St Helens would be his last competitive game. It was, though, a thought that had been lingering in the back of his mind. He still enjoyed playing rugby but it came at a cost. He was carrying more than his fair share of injuries and had become increasingly absent from matches. When he did play, it took him the best part of a week to recover from the discomfort and, of course, sometimes there were midweek fixtures to fulfil, in addition to attending training twice weekly. It was also a fact that Chris would celebrate his 35th birthday during the 1979/80 season:

> I didn't say to anybody after my last match about retiring at all. I went to a training session afterwards and it was then that I just suddenly decided. I just packed in and that was it. I went home and put my training gear down and said 'There's no need to wash that any more, I'm not going again!' Every night when I got home I was lying on the floor with one arm behind me trying to get rid of this pinched nerve in my neck that was sending pains up the back of my arm. I just felt battered. It was quite simple really. I didn't make an announcement I just said to myself 'I'm not training any more.'
>
> As a matter of fact, one of the things that really triggered me into retiring was when we played Featherstone Rovers at Salford on 1 September 1978. I always prided myself on my

defence, and a young lad called John Gilbert – a right centre – got the ball, looked at me, and just went round me, and nobody ever went round me! If they were faster than me I was always a yard outside them so they would come back inside. But he went round me with pure pace. I'd lasted 16 seasons but I was not moving as sharply any more. I thought to myself then: 'That's it! The body won't take anymore.'

There was a time at Salford when I never got injured and I never missed a match. My problems really started in the home match with Castleford in December 1971 when I did my cartilage. I moved to one side and my knee locked – the pain was terrible. I remember I threw the ball to somebody else and just went down. It seemed unreal at the time because people would say 'That's Chris Hesketh. He doesn't get hurt!' Jimmy Heywood – who was the skip man – and Ken Roberts – who was on the coaching staff – helped me off the field. I knew it was something really serious because I couldn't straighten my leg. I didn't know what it was at the time. But I was very fortunate in as much as I didn't get a lot of injuries in the best part of my playing life. Later on, my neck became really bad and I used to lie on the floor at home in a certain position to relieve the pain. I got that problem in a match against Dewsbury when somebody dropped me on to my shoulder and, to this day, it's never been right, although nothing like as bad as when I was playing because I was aggravating it all the time.

I had a groin injury as well! Groin injuries are bad because you're obviously running around and it is very painful. For many weeks and months I was going to Hope Hospital for painkilling injections in my groin. If it was a Friday night match at The Willows I'd go there about 4.30 pm and by the time of the kick-off at 7.30 pm I'd be all right. The next morning, of course, I couldn't move! They wouldn't let you do that these days because all you're doing is making it worse. Some people – probably quite rightly – said I played on too long and probably I did for my own personal good.

Of his 443 starts for Salford, he was selected 385 times in the centre – 47 on the right and 338 on the left – 48 at stand-off, eight on the wing and one each at full-back and loose-forward. 'It never worried me where I was picked to play' says Chris, 'although my body's got a preference for left centre rather than right, because I am right handed. I preferred to play at left centre, but to be honest it never really bothered me. You're going to be passing the ball a lot when you play hundreds of matches and within any match you're going to be going left or right. My natural position would be left centre but if they said to me "Play on the right" as I did in the 1972 World Cup, that's okay as well.'

It was mostly injuries that stopped Chris extending his international career beyond the 1974 tour. With the 1975 World Cup due to feature England and Wales, rather than Great Britain, the two countries were involved in a triangular tournament earlier that year that also included France. Chris, however, was not picked when the England team to meet France in Perpignan during January was announced. 'I'm a little disappointed' was his reaction at the time, 'however I expected changes and you've got to try players out. I've had a lot of football this past year, but I hope to come back into the international reckoning.' He got his wish, being picked for the next game, against Wales at Salford, the following month. It was also the first time he was given the England captaincy, but had to pull out following a late fitness check through his troublesome groin.

When the 1975 England World Cup squad was chosen for the trip to Australia and New Zealand in June, Chris's name was absent from the list. 'To be honest, I wasn't at all bothered' says Chris, 'You get to a stage when touring is not just about playing a lot of games of rugby, its about a lot of travelling, and being away from home. It's very, very tiring. I had already been there in 1974 and I suppose I could say it's even more wearing when you're the captain. Lads love going on tour but you never rest like you can at home.' Chris was picked for England again later in the year for a 'Special Challenge' match against Australia at Headingley on 1 November, but, once more, was forced to make a late withdrawal, this time through a bout of influenza.

A year later, England coach Peter Fox – who had taken over from Alex Murphy – was still keen to involve Chris in the international set-up, and turned up at The Willows on Sunday 5 December 1976 to watch him against Wakefield Trinity, where he impressed in the Reds' 22-13 victory, adding a try for good measure. The outcome was his inclusion in the England side to oppose Wales at Headingley on 29 January 1977. *The Observer*, in publishing the selected team on 19 December, wrote of Chris's inclusion under the headline 'Return Of An Old Soldier' saying 'Hesketh's tenacity and experience were the two qualities that influenced the England selectors.'

Whilst Chris would have dearly loved another crack at international rugby, he thought long and hard before writing a letter, dated 20 December 1976, to the England team manager, Harry Womersley, explaining that, whilst delighted to be asked, he did not feel he was fit enough to perform at that level. Womersley duly wrote back expressing his and Fox's regret at his withdrawal, adding 'I sincerely hope that the injury will clear up and you will be a contender for a place before the current season is completed.' Chris expanded on his decision in the *Manchester Evening News*, saying 'To play at international level demands total commitment and fitness. I wouldn't like to let down my team-mates or my country. I shall continue to play for Salford as long as I can, but I think the added effort of international rugby would be too much.' Chris's letter effectively drew a line under his international career, taking him out of contention for possible inclusion in the Great Britain side for the 1977 World Cup in Australasia, although he did not harbour any ambition to make such a long trip at that stage of his career.

For many former players, and particularly successful ones, moving into coaching is often the next logical step after retirement from 'active service.' During December 1975, Chris had told one rugby league writer 'I hope to stay in the game in a coaching or administrative capacity' but he was to have second thoughts. Looking back on it now, Chris says 'It was during my playing career when I said that and not at the end of it! During my career when I was playing rugby for Great Britain and for Lancashire, and I was playing for Wigan or Salford, it would have been my intention, then, to perhaps go back to Australia or New Zealand and coach, or possibly coach in England. But I already had a full-time job. I worked all the time – as most of the lads did – and I wanted to do well in that career, which I believe I have done. And the more I looked at the offers from Swinton and Barrow and Blackpool Borough, and whoever else it was, I was thinking "Hold on a minute! I'm risking a lot for a little here." Today, if I was 20 or 30 years younger and coaching Wigan or Leeds or somebody like that, I might have thought more seriously about it. There is a lot more money involved now.'

At the end of his time as a Salford player, Chris was courted by several clubs, including Barrow – who sent a deputation to The Willows on 29 September 1978 to watch him in a home match with Bradford Northern – Oldham and Swinton. There were also reports of interest from Wigan, following the departure of Vince Karalius in September 1979. Jack Bentley, in the *Daily Express*, wrote: 'Chris Hesketh yesterday emerged as favourite for the Wigan coaching post. All the signs are favourable for Hesketh, one of Wigan's best known and respected sons. And I know that Chris would favourably consider the job. To end his career as coach of the club where he began, in his hometown, would write a glorious finish to what has been something of a story-book rugby league life.'

I read that story too! To be honest nobody from Wigan ever approached me. If they had – and this goes for Salford as well – I would have given it serious consideration, as they are the two clubs that mean the most to me. But, apart from that, I was not really interested in becoming involved in coaching. I remember the Barrow chairman, Bill Oxley, coming to my house – which was then in Lowton – and asking would I go to Barrow as a player–coach. I talked it through with him but I told him 'No, I can't really handle that.' I was thinking its a long corridor up to Barrow and back and I couldn't do with all the extra driving.

At the back end of my playing days, when I was seriously thinking of packing it in, two blokes from Oldham came to my house to talk to me. I particularly remember it, because this big posh car pulled up outside. They asked me 'Would you be interested in coming to Oldham?' Whether that was as a player or player–coach I wouldn't swear on now, but I was not really interested.

Swinton's chairman Roy Fisk rang me and I met him at the Greyhound Hotel on the East Lancashire Road. I think it was December 1979. He said he wanted me at Swinton as coach or player–coach. The item of payment came up and he told me more or less what it was – I can't remember now exactly how much but it wasn't going to make me rich – and I went away and I thought 'Do I really want all that trouble for that amount as well as doing my job?' I was thinking about having to work all day and then driving across to Swinton in the evening, and I got back to him and said 'No, thank you.'

What Chris did eventually agree to, though, was to take over as the Blackpool Borough coach in March 1980. At the end of the previous season, Borough had shocked the rugby league world in gaining promotion to Division One but, as the 1979/80 term drew to a close, they were rooted to the bottom of the table and certain of relegation. The seaside club had already tried to recruit Chris as a player but, according to the club's official programme, he 'declined due to business commitments.' Not to be put off, Borough came back to him a week later, following the departure of their coach, Graham Rees, the former Salford, Swinton and St Helens forward. Again, according to the club's programme, 'Chris has agreed to take charge of the team for the rest of the season. If he finds that the time involved with the team can be coordinated with his business interests it is then hoped that next season the arrangement will become permanent. Whilst this may seem an odd state of affairs to some, it says an awful lot for the integrity and professionalism of Chris Hesketh, and an awful lot for the determination of Blackpool Borough to appoint a first class coach.'

It was Reg Parker, my 1974 tour manager, who asked me to go to Blackpool Borough as the coach. He was the chairman there at the time and I remember Roy Evans, who was loose forward at Wigan when I played there, was a director as well. I said I'd go to Blackpool until the end of the season, and I was in charge for the last six matches. The first one was on 30 March when we lost 13-0 to Castleford at home. We only won one match while I was there, which was the next when we beat York 19-0 at Borough Park on Good Friday. But I think we did very well when you look at the team we had although, to be fair, we had some fairly decent players. We had John Risman, the former Workington Town player, at full-back, Alan Fairhurst from Leigh at stand-off, Jim Molyneux – who used to be at Wigan – in the forwards, and there were a few from Salford like Tony Redford, Graham Mayor and John Corcoran.

One of the matches was against Bradford Northern – who went on to win the Division One Championship – at Borough Park on 6 April. We played very well in the first half and I was in the dressing room at half-time going around the players saying 'If we keep this up during the second half we can do these men.' We only lost 15-14, which was a miracle really. It was an incredible performance and I felt quite proud of them.

The last match was on 20 April – another home game – when we lost 22-1 to Wakefield Trinity. I went into the office afterwards to collect my money and said 'Well, thanks very much and I'll see you again some time.' And they said something like 'What do you mean?' I said 'That's it, I've finished now, it was until the end of the season.' 'No, no, we want you to stay.' I said 'No, I've finished. I said to Reg Parker I'll do it until the end of the season and that's it. I've got a job to go to. I work for a living and I can't keep coming up here every Tuesday and Thursday and at the weekend.' All I did it for was as a favour until the end of the season.

Chris's Blackpool experience was not, however, quite the last episode in his involvement with professional rugby league. The following season he was approached by Swinton – then coached by Frank Myler with Chris's former Salford colleague Peter Smethurst as his assistant – and persuaded to make a comeback. He signed for them on Thursday 11 September 1980 on a free transfer from Salford – who still held his registration despite not having played for 16 months – and was immediately selected for the Lions' next match three days later, ironically against Blackpool Borough, at Station Road. By Saturday – the day before the match – Chris had had second thoughts and contacted the club to say he had decided to stay retired. Swinton chairman Roy Fisk's reaction was that he was 'baffled and disappointed.' Chris, who had not accepted any payment to sign and claimed it was not a question of money, told the *Salford City Reporter*: 'I thought seriously about signing but did more soul searching afterwards. I have this long standing neck injury since I played for Salford and realised at my age, nearly 36, it wouldn't have been sensible to take any further risks.'

Consequently, the only games Chris has appeared in since finishing at Salford have been for 'good causes'. On 25 May 1983 he returned to The Willows turf to play for a team labelled '1974 Champions' against the current Salford line-up as part of the SOS – 'Save Our Salford' – fund, a campaign organised by supporters to clear some of the clubs debts. The current Salford team won 20-16, McNamara, in describing one passage of play, said 'The Champions build-up to their first try reads like a roll call of the greats – Ken Gill beginning the move, passing to centre Chris Hesketh, a strong run and there, surging up on his left, is full-back Paul Charlton, with Maurice Richards finishing off in classic style.'

It was over three years later – on Wednesday 20 August 1986 – before Chris laced his boots one last time, in an event organised to raise money for the relatives of former World Cup colleague Clive Sullivan who had, sadly, passed away the previous year. On an evening when a galaxy of stars turned out, the main feature was a combined Hull/Hull Kingston Rovers versus Great Britain XIII match. Chris – along with many other former 'greats' – lined up in a team called the International All Stars who took on the Humberside All Stars in a preliminary game. 'I got back home afterwards' says Chris, 'and my wife said "Chris, what's that?" I'd got a cut in my head and all my hair was matted. I had to go to hospital and have stitches!' In January 1973 Sullivan – having led England to their World Cup triumph over Australia in France two months before – had been the subject of television's famed 'This Is Your Life' series, presented in those days by Eamonn Andrews, and Chris was one of the guests. Although transmitted to the nation on 3 January, it was recorded five weeks earlier. Chris must have thought it was a 'wind up' when he heard Thames Television had booked him into the Clive Hotel, Hampstead, for an overnight stay on 29 November!

Chris has kept in touch with the sport in the years since his playing days but, apart from his brief spell as coach at Blackpool Borough, has not had any 'hands-on' involvement. Along with several famous Reds players of the past, he returned to The Willows for the first time on Sunday 14 October 1979 when Salford celebrated its centenary, taking part in the pre-match presentation prior to Salford's 16-16 draw with Widnes. Whenever he can, he still attends the annual Red Devils Association dinner – when the Lance Todd Trophy is presented – and British Rugby League Lions Association reunions. But the main focus for his energies has been his full-time job:

When I was still at Salford I got chatting to Brian Snape. We had played at Hull Kingston Rovers and, returning on the team coach, he said 'What do you do for a living?' and I replied 'I'm a rep.' I was working for the paintbrush company, LG Harris, who were based in Stoke Prior, Worcestershire, when I signed for Salford. He owned a plumbers' merchant called Fergusons, on Regent Road, Salford, and he said 'Do you fancy working for me?' I can't recall what money he offered me, but it must have been better than what I was on, and I went there. I used to unload the wagons with the lads; toilets, basins, everything! It kept me fit going up and down the stairs! I used to think to myself 'Why do they put all this heavy tackle upstairs in the back?' Because I worked for Brian Snape – although I never took advantage of him in any other way – it did help because I could have the afternoon off to go training for Great Britain or Lancashire and, in a way, it was good for Fergusons, particularly in the Salford area, having a so-called celebrity as a rep.

After I finished playing I went working as a sales representative for a company called FEB Limited in Swinton. They made building chemicals and I was there for about 11 years. Then I went to a firm called Thermalite

Blocks on Agecroft Road, near Pendlebury. They wanted a northern regional sales director. I applied for the job and I got it. They eventually got taken over by Marley Roof Tiles. I stayed with them for a while and then joined another builders merchant called Harcros, based in Bury, as their northern regional sales director. Unfortunately the north regional premises closed down leaving me with the option of moving to another regional area with them or leaving. I decided to leave and was quite fortunate because, within the same few weeks, I saw another job advertised with Eternit Clay Tiles, based in Keele, Staffordshire, and I became their northern regional sales manager. They later bought out Marley Roof Tiles, so, in a sense, I've gone full circle. I'm now working for what is known as Marley Eternit Limited, which has a head office at Coleshill, Warwickshire, as the national sales director for their Profiled Sheeting Division. It's a job that takes me all over the country and abroad on occasions as well, which is why it is so difficult for me to attend some rugby league functions whenever I get invited.

One of the saddest duties for Chris, since his rugby playing days, has been to attend the funerals of three former Salford colleagues; Peter Smethurst in 1989, Colin Dixon four years later, and Jim Hardicre – who was also chairman of the Red Devils Association for former Salford players and officials – in 2005. 'Peter was only 51' says Chris, 'I remember being at work and walking down this corridor at Harcros, and someone said to me "Have you heard about Peter Smethurst?" I said "What about him?" He replied "He's died". I was thinking to myself "Peter Smethurst can't be dead, because he'll never die." To me he was such a larger than life character, the type you thought would go on forever. Colin was also quite young. He was only 49. At his funeral, the church was overflowing and I remember, as they were walking the coffin past us, Jim Mills and myself just stood there crying our eyes out, and we weren't the only ones. Jim Hardicre was another sad loss and a great character to have known.'

Today, Chris still follows the game that he has loved all his life, although acknowledging that it has evolved into a sport that is vastly different to his playing days. He can also reflect on a rugby league career where he hit the heights but played strictly within the rules, never being sent off by a referee:

I've come close a couple of times! To be honest I never knowingly went to smack anybody. I'd want to hit them but I never went in with the intention of really hurting them. But there were two occasions when I thought I would get sent off. One was in front of the main stand at Salford and I remember Leeds were playing towards the club end. Syd Hynes came at me – we were great friends but big enemies on the field – and he sidestepped inside and it wasn't that I was intending to hit him but I just put my arm out and of course Syd hit it and he just went 'boing' and he was down. I looked at the referee and I thought 'I'm gone here!' but, to my relief, he didn't dismiss me. And the other time was at Workington. It was in the bottom corner of the ground where the players come out. It was a bad day, weather-wise, and, to be honest, I did commit a foul on somebody and I heard the referee blow his whistle and, again, I thought 'I'm going!' He called me over to him and he gave me a talking to. Looking back now, I can't remember who it was I fouled or even what I did, but I must admit at that time I was panicking.

I've watched Super League for a few years now on the television. To be honest I do find some of it is quite dire. I know it's a different game, but Les Bettinson would always say you run round a man, you don't run at him. All right if you're driving the ball away from your posts that's a different thing. One of my pet hates, is the Australian terminology we seem to use now; arm wrestle, muscling up, hit outs, the paddock, field goals, and so on. I just wish people would start talking proper English. This is our game!

I'm still a Salford supporter now. When I moved to Salford, Wigan were like Manchester United as far as rugby league was concerned, and it probably looked like a step down at the time. But, in actual fact, the next 10 or 12 years were marvellous. It turned round and Salford was the new Manchester United. It was a wonderful, wonderful time to be at the club. Players came and went, although they didn't come and go that much as we had quite a bit of stability. It wasn't just about the fact that we had a good team and were winning the Championship or the Floodlit Trophy or the Lancashire Cup or that I was playing for my county and country. There was a certain homeliness about Salford. Not only the surroundings, but the people too. We very rarely lost at home, and on Friday nights after the match you'd go in the Willows Variety Centre and there was a nice feeling about the whole thing. Don't get me wrong – they weren't all coming patting you on your back, because they're not that sort, but they wanted to talk to you and you'd want to talk to them. They'd say things like 'Chris, do you want a pint?' I've got a photograph taken in the club with a couple of the fans and referee Fred Lindop. You wouldn't see that happen now would you?

Since I stopped playing, people have often said to me 'Are you not involved in the game any more?' I say 'No'. Basically I got my head stuck into my job. I love my job and I'm not unhappy about being away from the game. I'm not a regular at functions because I can't always get to them through work. With all the amounts players can earn in Super League now, I get asked 'Don't you wish you were still playing today Chris, with all that money?' I always say 'No, I don't' because you couldn't buy the memories I've got of rugby league. I've not got memories of earning loads of money, but I've got memories of wonderful teams, great players, great supporters, great people, and some wonderfully happy, laughing, hilarious times with some of the funniest men I've ever known, and some of the most genuine straight forward people I've ever known. Salford has never been what you would call a wealthy city but the people I always found were just wonderful. I really mean that.

His career at Salford covered one of the most exciting periods in the club's history, supporters being treated to brilliant and spectacular rugby by some of the biggest and most glamorous stars ever to grace a rugby league field. Throughout it all, Chris provided a steadying influence; a dedicated and totally professionally minded player who combined a resolute defence with one of the most exciting, yet unorthodox sidesteps ever seen from a rugby player. Chris got his reward as captain of club, county and country and through the awarding of his MBE. The Salford fans got their reward through the privilege of seeing him play in that famous red jersey for 12 glorious seasons. As a player he was loved, respected and admired by fellow players, officials, coaching staff and supporters – a true Captain Courageous.

12

THE DREAM TEST MATCH

Inviting Chris to name his best-ever team from the players that he either played with or against during his 16-year professional career proved to be a challenge. After several days of deliberation, he eventually settled for the following two line-ups containing a combination of English, Welsh and Australian players. It is hard to disagree with Chris's assertion that either would have given any Test team a run for its money:

> It was very difficult to choose the two teams and there are many wonderful players that I was associated with over the years that have not been included. Despite my great admiration for my Salford colleague Kenny Gill, I picked Roger Millward and Bobby Fulton as my stand-offs because I think it is a big advantage at international level to have genuine pace in that position, whereas Kenny was a provider – and a wonderful one at that. There are also some wingmen that I have had the pleasure of partnering in the three-quarter line like Wigan's Trevor Lake – who was a wonderful finisher – and Salford's Maurice Richards, who I have also omitted. And then there was those wonderful Castleford half-backs Keith Hepworth and Alan Hardisty, and centre Syd Hynes and stand-off Mick Shoebottom, both of Leeds, as well as some truly great forwards that I have left out. But I could only pick 26 and just imagine the following two teams playing against each other – what a match that would have been!

Chris Hesketh's Dream Test Team I:

Paul Charlton (Salford, Workington Town, Blackpool Borough, Great Britain)

In my lifetime – and I can go back to seeing players like Jackie Cunliffe and Fred 'Punchy' Griffiths at Central Park in the 1950s as well as later full-backs like Ray Dutton of Widnes and the versatile John Holmes at Leeds – Paul Charlton stands out above them all. He was very unlucky not to go on the 1970 tour although he made up for that in 1974 and he was also in the 1972 World Cup winning team. As far as I am concerned, Paul was the absolute best attacking and defending full-back in my time.

Billy Boston (Wigan, Blackpool Borough, Great Britain)

Along with a lot of other people I thought Billy Boston was the best winger I'd ever seen. He was everybody's idol. He was and still is a wonderful person to know. I first saw Billy when I was just a young lad after he signed for Wigan in 1953. He was a lot quicker and slimmer in those days – although he was still quick when he got older – and nobody could ever lay a finger on him. He would go for 60 or 70 yards at a time. Billy was, to me, the best attacking winger ever but he was also a good defensive player as well. I never imagined when I was a youngster I would one day play alongside him.

Eric Ashton (Wigan, Great Britain)

My idol! Everything Eric Ashton did was classy. He looked classy, he acted classy and he played classy. Everything he did, those little back passes to Billy Boston, his sidestep, his pace, pure class. And he always presented himself well, a real gentleman.

Reg Gasnier (Sydney St George, Australia)

Reg Gasnier had every skill; speed, sidestep, tackling, the lot. I played against him for Lancashire at Salford in 1967 when he captained the Australian tourists, and he scored a try against us and it was just like a blur as he went over. Take your eyes off him for a second and he was gone. I did meet him once when I was on tour in Australia in 1970. With Gasnier, you're talking about a very high class performer who must rate with the best Aussies there's ever been. I know he's a legend in Australia.

John Atkinson (Leeds, Carlisle, Great Britain)

John Atkinson is, perhaps, not what you would describe as a classy winger, but he was a very fine finisher, one of the best I've known. He was a very fast, and also a very hard winger who never went back an inch. When I played with him for Great Britain, he was a great person to have as a member of your team. Not just as a winger, either, because he'd turn up all over the shop, if anything extra was required infield. He was as good a Test winger as I've ever come across. Along with Alan Smith on the other wing they made a magnificent strike partnership for Leeds and Great Britain.

Roger Millward (Castleford, Hull Kingston Rovers, Cronulla, Great Britain)

Roger Millward was a natural, a world class stand-off, and the most laid back man you'd ever meet. The Australians thought that Roger was the ultimate out-half when he toured there in 1970 and 1974, and he was!

Alex Murphy (St Helens, Leigh, Warrington, Great Britain)

The all time best scrum-half – league or union – as far as I am concerned. Alex Murphy was dominant, he was bossy, he was as sharp as a needle and he was brave. He had complete presence on the field and would always be chatting the referee up! He had wonderful acceleration and a real eye for an opening.

Brian McTigue (Wigan, Blackpool Borough, Great Britain)
Brian McTigue was very much an old style prop forward, typical of the 1950s and early 1960s era. He would take the ball in to the opposition, knowing that other people were around him in support to take those superb passes of his. He was a really skilful ball player and I know the Australians thought very highly off him when he toured there in 1958 and 1962.

Kevin Ashcroft (Dewsbury, Rochdale Hornets, Leigh, Warrington, Salford, Great Britain)
Perhaps a bit of a shock choice to some people, but I think Kevin Ashcroft was a very good hooker. He was also a very good talker on the field. When I was tour captain in 1974, if Kevin was playing in the team, he would help me out tremendously. As the captain, you're having to do all sorts of things on the field, as well as trying to win the match, and perform well yourself. But Kevin would run that pack for you. He was never frightened of voicing his opinion. I didn't necessarily agree with everything he said, but I had a lot of time and respect for him.

Cliff Watson (St Helens, Cronulla, Great Britain)
Cliff Watson was a Londoner who answered a St Helens advert for players in a Midlands newspaper. He turned out to be one of the hardest men I've ever played with, or against. He never took a step back and the Aussies had deep respect for him. I toured with him in 1970 and I know he was there with the 1966 party and, again, in 1968 for the World Cup. And, of course, he ended up playing in Australia and still lives there now. With Brian McTigue and Cliff Watson you're talking of two real old-style front-row craftsmen. You didn't

see Cliff Watson running out amongst the centres, he was in the middle where the real battle was and he did it to perfection.

Jim Thompson (Featherstone Rovers, Bradford Northern, Carlisle, Great Britain)

In any team that I ever played in, Jim Thompson would be the first name on the team sheet. He was, perhaps, the best tackler I ever came across and he would move along the line looking for work. With him in your team you'd go a long way towards solving your defensive problems, because once Jim got his hands on you, you were down. It is something that I always believed, in that, if you get your defence right first, you can do something about building the rest afterwards.

Arthur Beetson (Balmain, Eastern Suburbs, Parramatta, Hull Kingston Rovers, Australia)

Arthur Beetson was a big, hard man to play against and a good ball distributor. He was a very dominating forward and, possibly, the best in the world at his peak. I came up against him in the 1973 Tests in England and the 1974 series in Australia, as well as the 1972 World Cup. He went to Hull Kingston Rovers for a spell in 1968, which ended when he broke his leg against Hull on Christmas Day. Look at any Australian Test side and I don't think you'd find a wimp amongst them, and certainly not Arthur Beetson, because they soon get found out in Australia.

Johnny Raper (Newtown, Sydney St George, Australia)

Johnny Raper stood out as a world class loose forward, and I know the Australians rate him as one of their all-time greats in that position, although we had a couple of good 'uns around at that time with Vince Karalius at St Helens and Johnny Whiteley of Hull, who both toured in 1958. Like with

Reg Gasnier, I played against Raper in the Lancashire versus Australia match at Salford in 1967. Even on the muddy pitch that we had that night, his class stood out.

Chris Hesketh's Dream Test Team II:

Graeme Langlands (Sydney St George, Australia)
Graeme Langlands – who they used to call 'Changa' – was the Australian team captain and coach when I went out there in 1974. When you saw him come on to the field in his green and gold jersey you could see how proud he was, although, I have to say, I was very proud to be wearing the red, white and blue of Britain. He was a great player. Graham Eadie was also in contention as a full-back in 1974 but, whereas Eadie was the quick type of player who you could almost have played on the wing, Langlands was more of a specialist full-back. I particularly remember when we were both presented to the Australian Prime Minister, Gough Whitlam, before the first Test in Brisbane.

Bill Burgess (Barrow, Salford, Great Britain)
I loved watching Billy Burgess play, and I loved to be playing on the same team as him. To see Billy in full flight was something special. He always looked as if he was not running full out but, somehow, he used to glide past people. He was mesmerising and you never could predict which way he would go. I was always a very big admirer of his because he was a real class winger and I played alongside him for Lancashire before he joined Salford from Barrow. We missed him greatly at Salford after he was forced to retire through injury.

Alan Davies (Oldham, Wigan, Wakefield Trinity, Salford, Great Britain)
What can I say about Alan Davies? He had everything and he was

part of that wonderful Oldham team in the 1950s that Griff Jenkins coached. He was a big man for a centre, not so much in height, but he was broad. He had great skills, he had pace and was a great passer of the ball, and he played his rugby hard.

Mark Harris (Eastern Suburbs, North Sydney, Australia)

I played against Mark Harris a few times – most notably in the 1972 World Cup Final for Great Britain against Australia – and he was one handful! I can say that from real experience. Probably the fact that I've got this awful arthritic shoulder now is because I used to keep having to hit him with it! He was a big strong lad.

Clive Sullivan (Hull, Hull Kingston Rovers, Oldham, Doncaster, Great Britain)

Clive Sullivan featured strongly in my life and features strongly in my memories. I roomed with him on tour for a while and he was a cracking bloke to be with. He was a wonderful winger and, although most people probably don't realise it, another who was not afraid to mix it, when required, on the odd occasion. Sully was a class winger and he had great acceleration. It's a great shame he was taken from us when he was still comparatively young.

Bob Fulton (Manly-Warringah, Eastern Suburbs, Australia)

I wouldn't really call Bobby Fulton a stand-off because, to me, he was more of a midfield player and, of course, he often played for Australia in the centre. I came up against him in both the 1970 and 1972 World Cup Finals as well as the Tests in 1973 and 1974. He was another of those players you dare not take your eyes off. He was so alert and very quick to spot an opportunity.

Steve Nash (Featherstone Rovers, Salford, Rochdale Hornets, Mansfield Marksman, Great Britain)

I've got big memories of Stevie Nash. Not just playing in the same team at Salford but for Great Britain as well. He was one of the smallest men on the field and there was some big lads knocking about who would be running straight at him. But I never saw Nashy flinch, not once. As a matter of fact I've seen him tip big forwards up and drop them on the floor instead! If things weren't going right on the field, he was quick to tell you, but he was like a lot of us, he didn't like losing! He wasn't a lightning quick half-back but he was fast and he was like the seventh man in the Featherstone pack when he played for them. He would have to be in any team for me.

Dennis Hartley (Doncaster, Hunslet, Castleford, Great Britain)
Perhaps a surprise selection to some, but Dennis Hartley was a big man and exactly what you needed in a front row. He had everything that Castleford and Great Britain wanted at the time. I toured with him in 1970, and, believe me, you couldn't take on the Australians with a mini-prop! You had to have somebody that would stand there and face them. He was not afraid to mix it and if someone whacked him, the chances were he'd get his own back as some point! Dennis was an out-and-out prop forward, the type you had to have in any successful team.

Peter Flanagan (Hull Kingston Rovers, Hull, Great Britain)
Peter 'Flash' Flanagan was, to me, an extrovert in everything he did! But he was a hell of a good hooker and a great character to have around as well and you need a bit of that in any team. He was one of the first hookers that I can remember going to acting half-back and running away with the ball, and bringing players from wider out into the attack.

Bob O'Reilly (Parramatta, Penrith, Eastern Suburbs, Australia)
I played against Bob O'Reilly quite a few times. He was in the

Australia side in the 1973 and 1974 Test series and he played in the 1970 and 1972 World Cup Finals. He was another really big man, very fast and a good ball-player as well.

Colin Dixon (Halifax, Salford, Hull Kingston Rovers, Great Britain)
I think Colin Dixon could and should have played a lot more games for Great Britain than the 14 that he did. He was a pure second-row forward and you could stick him out in the line between the centres – as we often did at Salford – which confused the opposition. Once Dicko got rolling with the ball in his hands he was always very difficult to put down. I've seen him score tries from 40 and 50 yards and there's not many second-row men that do that.

Bob McCarthy (South Sydney, Canterbury-Bankstown, Australia)
Bob McCarthy was one of the first second-row forwards to stand out wide after the limited tackles rule was introduced into rugby league. To me he was like a big centre and, believe me, he had some pace. I played against him in the 1973 Tests in England and, of course, he got that vital try in the third Test in Australia in 1974. He was always a class act, rampaging and running all over the field. You had to defend well when he was around.

Malcolm Reilly (Castleford, Manly-Warringah, Great Britain)
Malcolm Reilly was one of the best ever in his position. He changed his game and became a different sort of loose forward who ran wider out. He had the number '13' on his back but he popped up all over the place, as he did for Castleford at Wembley in 1969 to make the try for Alan Hardisty which turned the match against us. I toured with Malcolm in 1970 and he made such a big impression with the Aussies that he ended up playing there with Manly the following year.

APPENDIX A

The Chris Hesketh Fact File
Club summary season-by-season (official matches only):

	Season	Apps	Tries	Points
Wigan	1963/64	8+0	4	12
	1964/65	10+3	2	6
	1965/66	26+8	9	27
	1966/67	30+2	13	39
	Total	**74+13**	**28**	**84**
Salford	1967/68	31+1	8	24
	1968/69	44	12	36
	1969/70	41	14	42
	1970/71	40	15	45
	1971/72	34	6	18
	1972/73	45	18	54
	1973/74	43	15	45
	1974/75	40+1	5	15
	1975/76	40	16	48
	1976/77	35	13	39
	1977/78	25+2	4	12
	1978/79	25+5	2	6
	Total	**443+9**	**128**	**384**

Career summary:

	Years	Apps	Tries	Points
Wigan	1963-67	74+13	28	84
Salford	1967-79	443+9	128	384
Great Britain*	1970-74	21+2	6	18
GB Under-24s	1965-66	0+2	0	0
England	1968-69	3	0	0
Lancashire	1967-74	13+2	3	9
1970 tour**	1970	12	8	24
1974 tour**	1974	11+3	2	6
	Total	**577+31**	**175**	**525**

(* includes Tests on 1970, 1974 tours and World Cup 1970, 1972) (** excludes Tests)

Honours List:

World Cup winner 1972, runner-up 1970

County Championship winner 1969/70, 1973/74, 1974/75

Rugby League Championship winner 1973/74, 1975/76

Rugby League Challenge Cup runner-up 1965/66, 1968/69

Premiership Trophy runner-up 1976

Players' No.6 Trophy runner-up 1972/73

Lancashire Cup winner 1966/67*, 1972/73, runner-up 1973/74, 1974/75*, 1975/76

BBC2 Floodlit Trophy winner 1974/75

Lancashire Shield runner-up 1963/64 ('A' team)

National Sevens runner-up 1969

East Lancashire Sevens winner 1969

Halifax Sevens winner 1968, 1975

Huddersfield Sevens winner 1968

Leeds Sevens winner 1968, 1969

Rochdale Hornets Sevens winner 1971

St Helens Sevens winner 1970

Wigan Sevens winner 1964, 1968, 1969

(* Not in team for Final but received medal)

Notable achievements:

Fourth in all-time appearances list for Salford

Tenth in all-time try scorers list for Salford

Most Great Britain Test appearances by a Salford player

Most tours by a Salford player since Second World War

Second in all-times list of Lancashire appearances by a Salford player

APPENDIX B

Chris Hesketh career record match-by-match

First team games only, including friendly fixtures, plus representative games and 7-a-side tournaments

Club matches are all League Championship fixtures unless stated

Number in right hand column indicates starting position (1 – full-back, 2 – right wing, 3 – right centre, 4 – left centre, 5 – left wing, 6 – stand-off, 13 – loose forward, 14 – substitute). No position is given for 7-a-side tournaments.

(Abbreviations: W – Won, L – Lost, D – Drawn, CC – Club Championship, CM – Captain Morgan Trophy, CPO – Championship Play-Off, F=Friendly, FT – BBC2 Floodlit Trophy, JP – Players' No.6 Trophy/John Player Trophy, LC – Lancashire Cup, PT – Premiership Trophy, RLC – Rugby League Challenge Cup, WC – World Cup, WD = Western Division Championship, nu – not used, t – try/tries, * – captain, **bold** type – home matches)

At Wigan:

1963/64 season:

17 Aug	**Warrington** (F)	L 5-31	6
30 Nov	Leigh (WD)	L 7-20	6
15 Feb	Liverpool City (WD)	W 12-7	4
30 Mar	**Hunslet**	W 31-4	6 (3t)
4 Apr	Hull	W 38-12	6 (t)
10 Apr	Castleford	L 14-24	6
13 Apr	Hunslet	W 33-11	6
17 Apr	**Halifax**	D 3-3	6
22 Apr	**St Helens**	L 13-22	3

1964/65 season:

3 Aug	Wigan Sevens	W	(2t)
15 Aug	Warrington (F)	W 9-8	6
22 Aug	Swinton	L 3-9	14 (nu)
14 Nov	**Widnes**	L 3-10	14
21 Nov	Oldham	W 18-9	1 (t)
28 Nov	**Halifax**	W 13-0	14
19 Dec	Whitehaven	W 15-3	2
26 Dec	**Leigh**	W 13-6	4 (t)
1 Jan	**Warrington**	L 8-15	4
9 Jan	Workington Town	W 8-5	4
16 Jan	**Swinton**	W 7-3	2
23 Jan	**Liverpool City**	W 8-5	4
13 Feb	**Salford**	W 16-4	4

12 Apr	Widnes	L 0-18	14
17 Apr	Warrington	W 28-3	6
19 Apr	Salford	W 17-2	6
1965/66 season:			
14 Aug	**Warrington** (F)	W 38-17	14 (nu)
18 Aug	Whitehaven	W 23-10	14 (t)
21 Aug	Widnes	W 12-2	14
23 Aug	**Liverpool City**	W 22-10	2 (t)
28 Aug	**Oldham**	L 8-23	5
30 Aug	Leigh	W 25-18	5
1 Sep	Liverpool City	W 13-12	6 (t)
4 Sep	**New Zealand** (tour)	L 12-17	6
11 Sep	**Whitehaven** (LC1)	W 25-23	4
16 Sep	Oldham (LC2)	L 13-28	6
18 Sep	**Hull Kingston R**	W 20-11	6 (t)
24 Sep	Castleford	W 12-9	6 (t)
28 Sep	Warrington (F)	L 5-9	6
2 Oct	**Castleford**	L 8-10	6
9 Oct	Blackpool Borough	W 43-19	5
16 Oct	**Swinton**	L 8-13	4
20 Oct	GREAT BRITAIN	W 12-5	14
	UNDER-24 v France (at Oldham)		
30 Oct	**Blackpool Borough**	W 51-2	1
13 Nov	Warrington	L 4-14	6
20 Nov	**Workington Town**	W 29-8	4
27 Nov	**Widnes**	W 9-8	3
11 Dec	**Barrow**	W 12-7	3
18 Dec	Wakefield Trinity	W 13-10	14 (nu)
1 Jan	**Warrington**	W 6-0	14 (nu)
8 Jan	Hull Kingston R	L 2-15	14
29 Jan	**Wakefield Trinity**	W 7-5	14
5 Feb	Workington Town	L 3-7	14 (nu)
12 Feb	Huddersfield	W 10-2	14 (nu)
19 Feb	**Whitehaven**	W 39-0	4 (t)
26 Feb	**Halifax** (RLC1)	W 8-4	14 (nu)
28 Feb	Rochdale Hornets	W 35-5	5 (t)
9 Mar	Swinton	W 25-7	14
12 Mar	Barrow	W 22-8	4
15 Mar	Salford	W 36-8	4
19 Mar	**Whitehaven** (RLC2)	W 40-6	3 (t)
26 Mar	**St Helens**	W 17-8	14
6 Apr	Bradford N (RLC3)	W 15-6	14 (nu)
8 Apr	St Helens	L 10-17	14
9 Apr	**Huddersfield**	W 7-2	3
11 Apr	**Salford**	W 15-7	6
15 Apr	**Rochdale Hornets**	W 25-12	2 (t)
18 Apr	**Leigh**	W 17-7	2
23 Apr	Leeds (RLCsf at Huddersfield)	W 7-2	14
30 Apr	**Widnes** (CPO1)	W 27-10	14 (nu)
7 May	**Leeds** (CPO2)	W 22-5	14 (nu)
14 May	**Halifax** (CPOsf)	L 12-25	14 (nu)
21 May	St Helens (RLCf at Wembley)	L 2-21	14 (nu)
1966/67 season:			
6 Aug	Wigan Sevens	L (in s-f)	
12 Aug	Warrington (F)	L 8-10	6

17 Aug	Whitehaven	L 0-16	6
20 Aug	**Halifax**	L 22-34	1 (t)
24 Aug	Leigh	L 9-18	6
27 Aug	Wakefield Trinity	L 7-19	4
29 Aug	**Leigh**	W 18-13	4 (t)
3 Sep	Leigh (LC1)	W 18-4	4
6 Sep	Blackpool Borough	L 10-20	4 (t)
10 Sep	**Barrow**	W 24-14	14 (nu)
14 Sep	**St Helens** (LC2)	W 11-9	6
17 Sep	Leeds	L 25-38	14 (nu)
24 Sep	**Workington Town**	W 28-16	6
30 Sep	Oldham	W 16-15	1
8 Oct	**Swinton**	L 6-16	14
14 Oct	Barrow	W 15-13	14
5 Nov	**Wakefield Trinity**	L 13-15	6
12 Nov	**Whitehaven**	W 40-0	2 (t)
19 Nov	Halifax	W 9-8	14 (nu)
26 Nov	GREAT BRITAIN	L 4-7	14
	UNDER-24 v France (at Bayonne, France)		
16 Dec	Widnes	W 20-7	5 (t)
26 Dec	St Helens	L 3-8	5
27 Dec	**Salford**	W 28-11	5 (t)
2 Jan	**Warrington**	W 17-5	5 (2t)
14 Jan	Workington Town	L 8-9	5
28 Jan	**Widnes**	W 46-2	5 (2t)
4 Feb	Warrington (RLC1)	D 19-19	5 (t)
8 Feb	**Warrington** (RLC1r)	W 20-3	5
11 Feb	Huddersfield	W 10-8	6
18 Feb	**Leeds**	L 7-17	6
25 Feb	**Salford** (RLC2)	L 6-18	5
3 Mar	Rochdale Hornets	W 15-12	5 (t)
8 Mar	Swinton	L 11-14	5 (t)
18 Mar	**Oldham**	L 8-20	5
24 Mar	**St Helens**	L 7-21	5
25 Mar	Warrington	L 9-12	5
27 Mar	Salford	L 4-17	5
5 Apr	**Liverpool City**	W 24-7	5

At Salford:
1966/67 season:

11 June	Halifax Sevens	L (in 1st rd)	(t)

1967/68 season:

11 Aug	Wakefield Trinity (F)	W 29-6	3
19 Aug	Wigan (LC1)	W 18-14	3
21 Aug	Barrow	L 20-23	3
25 Aug	Castleford	L 14-21	6
28 Aug	**Swinton**	W 17-8	3 (t)
1 Sep	**St Helens**	L 3-15	3
4 Sep	Workington T (LC2)	L 0-33	3
8 Sep	Halifax	L 18-27	4
12 Sep	LANCASHIRE v Cumberland	W 19-6	3
	(at Workington)		
15 Sep	**Castleford**	L 14-19	6
20 Sep	**Rochdale Hornets**	W 30-4	4
25 Sep	Leigh	L 9-15	4
29 Sep	**Liverpool City**	W 18-5	4 (2t)

3 Oct	**Leigh** (FT1)	L 3-5	4
7 Oct	Whitehaven	W 10-0	5
11 Oct	LANCASHIRE v Australia (at Salford)	L 2-14	3
17 Oct	**Whitehaven**	W 23-7	4 (3t)
20 Oct	**Oldham**	W 12-6	2
28 Oct	Workington Town	L 8-13	4
3 Nov	**Featherstone Rovers**	L 11-12	4
13 Nov	Oldham	W 4-0	5
17 Nov	**Halifax**	W 14-3	14
24 Nov	St Helens	W 7-4	4
1 Dec	**Widnes**	W 15-3	4
22 Dec	Widnes	W 14-0	4
26 Dec	Batley	W 9-7	4
29 Dec	**Workington Town**	W 14-5	4
1 Jan	**Blackpool Borough**	W 17-0	4 (t)
7 Jan	Featherstone Rovers	W 10-9	4
19 Jan	**Barrow**	W 6-5	4
29 Mar	**Wigan**	W 15-13	4
5 Apr	**Great Britain** (F)	L 5-20	4 (t)
12 Apr	Blackpool Borough	W 18-4	4 (t)
13 Apr	Swinton	L 17-20	4
15 Apr	Wigan	L 14-25	4
19 Apr	Castleford (CPO1)	L 15-47	4
5 May	**Cavaillon** (F)	W 43-0	4 (t)
19 May	Huddersfield Sevens	W	(2t)
25 May	Leeds Sevens	W	(5t)
26 May	Halifax Sevens	W	(2t)
29 May	Hull Kingston R (F, at Jedburgh, Scotland)	L 33-36	1
1 Jun	Bradford Northern (F, at Abertillery, Wales)	L 22-46	1

1968/69 season:

3 Aug	Wigan Sevens	W	(2t)
14 Aug	Bradford Northern	W 11-5	4
16 Aug	**Hull**	W 19-2	4
21 Aug	Widnes	L 9-21	4
24 Aug	Wakefield Trinity	L 12-31	4
27 Aug	**Bradford Northern**	W 18-12	3
2 Sep	**Swinton**	L 3-11	3
6 Sep	**Warrington** (LC1)	W 14-3	3 (t)
15 Sep	Doncaster	W 18-12	3 (t)
20 Sep	**Whitehaven**	W 18-7	3
22 Sep	Whitehaven (LC2)	W 17-4	3 (2t)
25 Sep	LANCASHIRE v Yorkshire (at Craven Park, Hull)	L 5-10	14 (t)
28 Sep	Wigan	L 11-18	3
1 Oct	Leeds (FT1)	L 19-24	4
4 Oct	**St Helens**	D 10-10	4
9 Oct	**Oldham** (LCsf)	L 9-12	4
12 Oct	Whitehaven	W 21-2	6
18 Oct	**Rochdale Hornets**	L 7-10	3
30 Oct	**Oldham**	W 4-2	4
1 Nov	Warrington	L 8-12	4
6 Nov	LANCASHIRE v Cumberland (at St Helens)	W 24-19	3
7 Nov	ENGLAND v Wales (at Salford)	L 17-24	4
8 Nov	**Workington Town**	L 10-18	4
22 Nov	**Barrow**	D 14-14	5

29 Nov	Leigh	W 20-5	5 (t)
6 Dec	**Doncaster**	W 44-2	4 (t)
20 Dec	**Wakefield Trinity**	W 17-3	4
1 Jan	**Blackpool Borough**	W 39-8	4
9 Jan	East Lancashire 7s (at Salford)	W	(t)
10 Jan	**Leigh**	D 6-6	4
18 Jan	Oldham	L 12-22	5
25 Jan	**Batley** (RLC1)	W 17-2	4
27 Jan	Hull	D 5-5	6
31 Jan	Huyton ('away' match at Salford)	W 18-5	5
6 Feb	National Sevens Final (at Swinton)	L (in final)	(t)
23 Feb	**Workington** (RLC2)	W 12-5	5
2 Mar	**Widnes** (RLC3)	W 20-7	4 (t)
15 Mar	Rochdale Hornets	W 23-8	4 (t)
22 Mar	Warrington (RLCsf at Wigan)	W 15-8	4
28 Mar	Barrow	W 11-8	4
1 Apr	**Widnes**	W 29-3	4 (t)
4 Apr	Blackpool Borough	W 49-7	4 (t)
5 Apr	Swinton	W 19-3	4 (t)
7 Apr	**Wigan**	W 37-5	4 (t)
11 Apr	**Huyton**	L 5-8	4
14 Apr	Workington Town	L 4-5	4
27 Apr	**York** (CPO1)	W 13-7	4
3 May	Wigan (CPO2)	W 26-21	4
10 May	Leeds (CPOsf)	L 12-22	4
17 May	Castleford (RLCf at Wembley)	L 6-11	4
26 May	Leeds Sevens	W	
1969/70 season:			
19 Jul	Wigan Sevens	W	(2t, g)
10 Aug	Huyton	W 60-5	4 (2t)
16 Aug	Wigan (LC1)	L 9-25	4
19 Aug	Oldham	W 20-11	4 (t)
30 Aug	Rochdale Hornets	L 10-15	4
1 Sep	**Swinton**	W 8-5	4
3 Sep	LANCASHIRE v Yorkshire (at Salford)	W 14-12	3
5 Sep	**Warrington**	W 20-13	4
10 Sep	**Wigan**	L 4-14	4
12 Sep	Hull Kingston Rovers	L 5-12	4
19 Sep	**Workington Town**	L 6-22	4
24 Sep	LANCASHIRE v Cumberland (at Workington)	W 30-10	3
26 Sep	**Huyton**	W 32-3	4 (2t)
3 Oct	**Rochdale Hornets**	W 41-0	4 (t)
10 Oct	Warrington	W 14-10	4
15 Oct	**Leigh**	W 15-5	4
18 Oct	ENGLAND v Wales (at Headingley)	W 40-23	4
21 Oct	**Castleford** (FT1)	L 12-16	4 (t)
25 Oct	ENGLAND v France (at Wigan)	D 11-11	4
29 Oct	**St Helens**	W 16-12	6 (2t)
31 Oct	Widnes	W 19-2	6
7 Nov	**Batley**	W 28-9	4
22 Nov	Whitehaven	W 13-7	4 (t)
28 Nov	**Wakefield Trinity**	W 17-12	4 (t)
13 Dec	**Hull Kingston R**	L 7-22	4
21 Dec	Workington Town	W 6-4	4
26 Dec	**Barrow**	W 14-7	4

1 Jan	**Blackpool Borough**	W 36-14	4
2 Jan	**Whitehaven**	W 7-2	6
11 Jan	Wakefield Trinity	L 5-7	6
16 Jan	**Castleford**	L 7-12	4
27 Jan	St Helens	W 16-15	4 (t)
30 Jan	Widnes	W 19-7	4
8 Feb	Featherstone (RLC1)	W 7-2	4
22 Feb	**Huddersfield** (RLC2)	D 0-0	4
26 Feb	Huddersf'ld (RLC2 replay at Swinton) ('home' match)	W 11-5	4
27 Feb	**Oldham**	W 30-3	4 (t)
1 Mar	Leigh	D 6-6	4
7 Mar	Castleford (RLC3)	L 0-15	4
15 Mar	ENGLAND v France (at Toulouse, France)	L 9-14	14 (nu)
20 Mar	Castleford	L 5-20	6
27 Mar	Blackpool Borough	W 41-11	4
28 Mar	Swinton	L 5-12	4
30 Mar	Wigan	L 11-24	4
12 Apr	Batley	W 23-0	4
19 Apr	**Hull** (CPO1)	W 11-4	4 (t)
24 Apr	Hull KR (CPO2)	L 16-27	4

1970 Great Britain tour:
In Australia:

22 May	Northern Territory (at Darwin)	W 35-12	4 (2t)
26 May	Central Queensland (at Rockhampton)	W 30-2	3
7 Jun	Toowoomba (at Toowoomba)	W 37-13	3
10 Jun	Brisbane (at Brisbane)	W 28-7	4
14 Jun	Monaro (at Queanbeyan)	W 34-11	4 (t)
21 Jun	Western Australia (at Bathurst)	W 40-11	4
23 Jun	Sydney Colts (at Woolooware)	W 26-7	4
27 Jun	Newcastle (at Newcastle)	W 49-16	3
5 Jul	Southern New South Wales (at Wollongong)	W 24-11	4 (t)

In New Zealand:

8 Jul	Northern XIII (at Tokoroa)	W 42-17	4 (t)
14 Jul	Wellington (at Wellington)	W 60-8	4 (2t)
21 Jul	West Coast (at Greymouth)	W 57-2	3 (t)
25 Jul	New Zealand (3rd test at Auckland)	W 33-16	3 (t)

1970/71 season:

1 Aug	St Helens Sevens	W	(2t)
14 Aug	Keighley (F)	W 43-17	4
21 Aug	Hull Kingston Rovers	L 11-13	4
29 Aug	Oldham (LC1)	W 35-12	4 (2t)
31 Aug	**Swinton**	W 30-4	4
4 Sep	Wigan	L 7-13	4
9 Sep	**Castleford**	L 11-13	4
11 Sep	**Widnes**	L 8-13	4
13 Sep	Wigan (LC2)	D 12-12	4
16 Sep	Castleford	W 36-6	4 (2t)
19 Sep	Bradford Northern	W 25-9	4
20 Sep	Wigan (LC2 replay)	L 6-32	4
23 Sep	Leigh	L 14-20	4
25 Sep	**Featherstone Rovers**	W 45-7	4
30 Sep	Leigh	L 7-19	4

4 Oct	Huddersfield	W 10-8	4
9 Oct	Hull Kingston R	W 20-0	3
24 Oct	GREAT BRITAIN v Australia (WC at Headingley)	W 11-4	14 (nu)
28 Oct	GREAT BRITAIN v France (WC at Castleford)	W 6-0	14 (nu)
31 Oct	GREAT BRITAIN v New Zealand (WC at Swinton)	W 27-17	4 (t)
7 Nov	GREAT BRITAIN v Australia (WCf at Headingley)	L 7-12	14
11 Nov	LANCASHIRE v Cumberland (at Barrow)	W 28-5	4 (t)
14 Nov	Whitehaven	W 10-4	3 (t)
20 Nov	**St Helens**	L 0-4	3
29 Nov	Warrington	W 50-0	3 (t)
4 Dec	**Whitehaven**	W 33-20	3
12 Dec	Hull	D 12-12	3
26 Dec	**Barrow**	W 21-11	3 (t)
10 Jan	Wakefield Trinity	L 7-14	3
15 Jan	**Warrington**	W 40-15	3
24 Jan	Wakefield T (RLC1)	D 6-6	3
27 Jan	**Wakefield T** (RLC1 replay)	W 15-8	3
29 Jan	**Leeds**	L 4-42	3
7 Feb	GREAT BRITAIN v France (at Toulouse, France)	L 8-16	14
12 Feb	**Hull**	W 24-5	4 (t)
21 Feb	**Warrington** (RLC2)	W 20-9	4 (t)
24 Feb	LANCASHIRE v Yorkshire (at Castleford)	L 8-34	4
27 Feb	Leeds	L 13-24	6
6 Mar	Castleford (RLC3)	L 8-9	4
14 Mar	Featherstone Rovers	W 43-24	4
17 Mar	GREAT BRITAIN v France (at St Helens)	W 24-2	3
19 Mar	**Bradford Northern**	W 23-2	4 (t)
26 Mar	**Huddersfield**	W 17-5	4 (t)
30 Mar	**Rochdale Hornets**	W 18-9	4 (t)
9 Apr	Barrow	W 20-16	4 (t)
10 Apr	Swinton	W 23-20	4 (2t)
12 Apr	**Wigan**	W 16-7	6
16 Apr	Widnes	L 5-17	4
25 Apr	**Halifax** (CPO1)	W 33-3	4
1 May	Leeds (CPO2)	L 22-37	4
29 May	Leeds Sevens	L (in 1st rd)	

1971/72 season:

25 Jul	Wakefield Sevens (exhibition game)	W	(t)
27 Jul	Oldham (F)	W 35-8	4 (t)
30 Jul	**St Helens** (F)	W 28-13	4
31 Jul	Rochdale Sevens	W	(2t)
8 Aug	**Workington T** (LC1)	W 46-5	4 (t)
15 Aug	Swinton (LC2)	L 11-20	4
20 Aug	**Warrington**	W 8-6	4
24 Aug	**Huyton**	W 53-13	4
28 Aug	Halifax	W 45-2	4
30 Aug	**Swinton**	W 34-9	4
5 Sep	Huyton	W 18-7	4
7 Sep	Huddersfield	W 37-4	6 (t)
12 Sep	Warrington	W 15-13	6
17 Sep	**Leeds**	W 27-2	6

25 Sep	GREAT BRITAIN v New Zealand (1st test at Salford)	L 13-18	4 (t)
29 Sep	LANCASHIRE v Yorkshire (at Leigh)	L 22-42	4°
2 Oct	St Helens	L 12-23	6
10 Oct	Wakefield Trinity	W 25-5	4
16 Oct	GREAT BRITAIN v New Zealand (2nd test at Castleford)	L 14-17	4
19 Oct	**Rochdale H** (FT1)	L 15-17	4
22 Oct	**New Zealand** (tour)	W 31-30	4
24 Oct	**Hull**	W 17-7	4 (t)
30 Oct	Leeds	L 5-34	4
6 Nov	GREAT BRITAIN v New Zealand (3rd test at Headingley)	W 12-3	3
7 Nov	**Batley**	W 21-3	4
14 Nov	Hull KR (JP1)	L 14-17	4
21 Nov	Workington Town	L 5-9	6
26 Nov	**Warrington** (Players' No.6 top-tries contest)	W 38-7	4 (t)
5 Dec	Dewsbury	L 17-22	4 (t)
10 Dec	**Castleford**	W 25-9	4
5 Mar	Hull	L 14-22	4
10 Mar	**Workington Town**	W 28-0	4
17 Mar	Castleford	L 12-19	4
24 Mar	**St Helens**	L 0-7	4
31 Mar	Swinton	W 2-0	4
3 Apr	Wigan	W 13-10	4
7 Apr	**Dewsbury**	W 20-9	4
9 Apr	Huddersfield	W 14-9	4
16 Apr	Keighley	W 35-12	4
23 Apr	**Dewsbury** (CPO1)	W 23-7	4 (t)
30 Apr	Wigan (CPO2)	W 21-9	4
5 May	Leeds (CPOsf)	L 0-10	4
1972/73 season:			
4 Aug	**Dewsbury** (F)	L 14-15	4
11 Aug	**St Helens** (F)	D 12-12	4
19 Aug	**Leeds**	L 10-15	6
23 Aug	Featherstone Rovers	L 15-27	6 (t)
26 Aug	Whitehaven	W 32-17	3 (t)
28 Aug	**Swinton**	L 8-13	3 (t)
1 Sep	**Oldham** (LC1)	W 41-17	4
9 Sep	Leeds	L 10-19	4 (t)
15 Sep	**Rochdale H** (LC2)	W 46-13	4 (t)
17 Sep	Leigh	W 27-16	4
24 Sep	Barrow (JP1)	W 17-2	4
27 Sep	LANCASHIRE v Cumberland (at Warrington)	W 26-16	14
29 Sep	**Huyton**	W 62-10	4 (2t)
3 Oct	Oldham (FT1)	L 8-12	4
6 Oct	Wigan (LCsf)	W 14-2	4 (t)
8 Oct	Blackpool Borough	W 37-10	4
11 Oct	LANCASHIRE v Yorkshire (at Castleford)	L 18-32	14 (nu)
13 Oct	Blackpool Borough	W 43-13	4 (2t)
18 Oct	GREAT BRITAIN v Oldham (F, at Oldham)	L 15-18	3
21 Oct	Swinton (LCf at Warrington)	W 25-11	4
29 Oct	GREAT BRITAIN v Australia (WC at Perpignan, France)	W 27-21	3

1 Nov	GREAT BRITAIN v France (WC at Grenoble, France)	W 13-4	3
4 Nov	GREAT BRITAIN v New Zealand (WC at Pau, France)	W 53-19	3 (t)
11 Nov	GREAT BRITAIN v Australia (WCf at Lyon, France)	D 10-10	3
17 Nov	Warrington	L 11-16	4
19 Nov	**New Zealand** (tour)	W 50-4	4
24 Nov	**Dewsbury** (JP2)	W 19-3	4 (t)
26 Nov	**Workington Town**	W 27-10	4
1 Dec	**Barrow**	W 51-10	4
10 Dec	**Bradford N** (JP3)	W 39-2	4
13 Dec	Oldham	W 14-12	4
15 Dec	Leigh	W 18-2	4 (t)
24 Dec	Bradford Northern	W 19-11	4
26 Dec	Workington Town	W 12-3	4
30 Dec	Hull KR (JPsf)	W 15-13	4
3 Jan	**Bradford Northern**	W 30-4	4 (2t)
7 Jan	Rochdale Hornets	W 13-11	4
12 Jan	**Featherstone Rovers**	W 16-12	4
28 Jan	Featherstone (RLC1)	L 11-18	4
2 Feb	**Whitehaven**	W 25-7	4 (t)
11 Feb	Barrow	W 28-10	4
23 Feb	St Helens	W 15-10	4
7 Mar	Widnes	W 18-9	4 (t)
9 Mar	Dewsbury	W 15-7	4
16 Mar	St Helens	L 4-21	4
24 Mar	Leeds (JPf at Huddersfield)	L 7-12	4
30 Mar	**Warrington**	L 7-10	4
16 Apr	**Widnes**	W 17-7	4
13 Apr	**Oldham**	W 18-10	4 (t)
15 Apr	Dewsbury	L 7-14	4
17 Apr	Wigan	L 6-23	4
20 Apr	Swinton	W 29-11	6 (t)
23 Apr	**Wigan**	W 15-3	6
29 Apr	**Rochdale H** (CPO1)	L 10-14	6
23 May	Swinton (F)	W 27-23	4 (t)
1973/74 season:			
3 Aug	**Dewsbury** (F)	W 25-6	4 (t)
10 Aug	St Helens (F)	W 18-15	6
11 Aug	Wigan Sevens	L (in 1st rd)	
17 Aug	**Leigh**	W 31-4	6
25 Aug	Bramley	W 14-7	4
31 Aug	**Widnes** (LC1)	W 12-11	6
5 Sep	LANCASHIRE v Cumbria (at Barrow)	W 18-6	4
7 Sep	**Featherstone Rovers**	W 34-4	4 (t)
14 Sep	**Rochdale H** (LC2)	W 24-3	4
16 Sep	**Doncaster** (JP1)	W 47-17	4 (3t)
19 Sep	LANCASHIRE v Yorkshire (at Widnes)	W 17-15	4°
23 Sep	Widnes	W 23-10	4
25 Sep	Whitehaven (LCsf)	W 23-9	4
28 Sep	Hull Kingston Rovers	W 24-2	4
30 Sep	**Australia** (tour)	L 12-15	4
5 Oct	**Castleford**	W 16-5	4
13 Oct	Wigan (LCf at Warrington)	L 9-19	4

19 Oct	**Wigan**	W 8-4	4
23 Oct	**Warrington** (FT1)	W 26-4	4
28 Oct	Warrington	L 13-20	4 (t)
3 Nov	GREAT BRITAIN v Australia	W 21-12	4
	(1st test at Wembley)	W 21-12	4
6 Nov	Widnes (CM1)	W 32-9	4
9 Nov	Whitehaven	W 15-3	4
18 Nov	Workington T (CM2)	L 5-10	4
20 Nov	Widnes (FT2)	L 11-15	4
24 Nov	GREAT BRITAIN v Australia	L 6-14	4
	(2nd test at Headingley)		
1 Dec	GREAT BRITAIN v Australia	L 5-15	4
	(3rd test at Warrington)		
9 Dec	**Whitehaven**	W 52-5	4 (3t)
16 Dec	**Leeds** (JP2)	L 4-17	4
26 Dec	**Dewsbury**	W 39-2	4
1 Jan	**Oldham**	W 15-12	4
6 Jan	Castleford	W 16-11	4
12 Jan	**Bramley**	W 14-10	4
13 Jan	**Wakefield Trinity**	W 22-7	4
20 Jan	GREAT BRITAIN v France	W 24-5	4
	(at Grenoble, France)		
27 Jan	**St Helens**	L 11-12	4
3 Feb	**Oldham** (RLC1)	W 26-12	4 (2t)
10 Feb	**Widnes**	W 19-7	4 (t)
17 Feb	GREAT BRITAIN v France (at Wigan)	W 29-0	4
23 Feb	Leeds (RLC2)	L 6-10	4
3 Mar	**Hull Kingston R**	W 23-22	4 (t)
10 Mar	**Rochdale Hornets**	W 24-16	4
17 Mar	**Leeds**	W 61-13	4 (t)
19 Mar	St Helens	D 19-19	6
31 Mar	Wakefield Trinity	W 32-13	6
2 Apr	Leeds	L 5-7	6
7 Apr	Featherstone Rovers	L 16-27	4
9 Apr	**Warrington**	W 21-13	4 (t)
12 Apr	Leigh	W 24-21	4
13 Apr	Oldham	L 2-4	4
15 Apr	Wigan	W 21-12	4
21 Apr	**Bradford N** (CC1)	D 16-16	4 (t)
25 Apr	Bradford N (CC1 replay)	L 8-17	4

1974 Great Britain tour:
In Australia:

26 May	Darwin (at Darwin)	W 41-2	4°
30 May	North Queensland(at Cairns)	W 30-5	14°
2 Jun	Central Queensland (at Rockhampton)	W 38-0	3° (t)
6 Jun	Ipswich (at Ipswich)	W 36-8	3°
9 Jun	Queensland (at Brisbane)	W 13-12	4°
15 Jun	Australia (1st test at Brisbane)	L 6-12	4°
18 Jun	Brisbane (at Brisbane)	L15-20	4°
23 Jun	Northern Division (at Tamworth)	W 38-14	4° (t)
26 Jun	Western Division (at Orange)	W 25-10	4°
29 Jun	New South Wales (at Sydney)	L 9-13	4°
6 Jul	Australia (2nd test at Sydney)	W 16-11	4°
7 Jul	Monaro (at Queanbeyan)	W 34-7	3°
10 Jul	Riverina (at Wagga Wagga)	W 36-10	14°

| 13 Jul | Newcastle (at Newcastle) | W 24-14 | 14° |
| 20 Jul | Australia (3rd test at Sydney) | L 18-22 | 4° |

In New Zealand:

27 July	New Zealand (1st test at Auckland)	L 8-13	4°
30 July	Maoris (at Rotorua)	W 19-16	4°
4 Aug	New Zealand (2nd test at Christchurch)	W 17-8	6° (t)
10 Aug	New Zealand (3rd test at Auckland)	W 20-0	6° (t)
13 Aug	Auckland (at Auckland)	L 2-11	6°

1974/75 season:

25 Aug	Keighley	L 7-11	6°
26 Aug	**Halifax**	W 37-0	6°
6 Sep	**Featherstone Rovers**	L 11-12	6°
8 Sep	**Huyton** (LC2)	W 17-15	6°
15 Sep	York	W 24-14	13°
18 Sep	LANCASHIRE v Cumbria (at Warrington)	W 29-4	4°
20 Sep	**Dewsbury**	W 29-13	3° (2t)
25 Sep	LANCASHIRE v Yorkshire (at Keighley)	L 14-20	4° (t)
27 Sep	**Castleford** (JP1)	W 36-5	3° (2t)
2 Oct	**Keighley**	W 45-2	3°
6 Oct	Widnes	W 8-7	3°
11 Oct	**Workington** (LCsf)	W 17-10	3°
16 Oct	LANCASHIRE v Yorkshire (at Widnes)	W 29-11	3° (t)
19 Oct	Wigan	L 8-14	3°
25 Oct	**York**	W 42-15	3°
8 Nov	**Bramley** (JP2)	W 14-9	14°
12 Nov	St Helens (FT2)	W 11-7	6°
15 Nov	**Castleford**	W 13-10	3°
23 Nov	Leeds	L 15-28	3°
29 Nov	**Warrington**	W 11-7	3°
3 Dec	**Hull KR** (FTsf)	W 27-10	3°
7 Dec	Hull KR (JP3)	L 17-25	3°
15 Dec	Bradford Northern	L 5-14	3°
17 Dec	**Warrington** (FTf)	D 0-0	3°
22 Dec	Bramley	W 15-8	3°
26 Dec	**Widnes**	W 10-9	3°
29 Dec	**St Helens**	L 0-14	3°
1 Jan	**Rochdale Hornets**	W 18-0	3°
5 Jan	Featherstone Rovers	L 12-18	3°
10 Jan	**Wakefield Trinity**	L 6-16	1°
19 Jan	Warrington	L 2-7	4°
24 Jan	**Castleford**	D 11-11	4°
28 Jan	Warrington (FTf replay)	W 10-5	4°
2 Feb	St Helens	L 5-18	4°
9 Feb	Featherstone (RLC1)	W 17-7	4°
23 Feb	**Leeds** (RLC2)	L 12-17	4°
7 Mar	Castleford	W 15-12	4° (t)
11 Mar	**Bradford Northern**	L 7-9	4°
21 Mar	**Bramley**	W 28-8	4°
28 Mar	Rochdale Hornets	L 9-18	4°
31 Mar	**Wigan**	L 20-30	4°
20 Apr	Halifax	W 13-4	4°
27 Apr	Widnes (PT1)	W 20-12	4°
29 Apr	Wigan (PT2)	L 17-35	4°
30 Apr	France XIII (F, at Marseilles)	L 13-23	4° (t)

| 26 May | Leeds Sevens | L (in 1st rd) | (t) |
| 1 Jun | Halifax Sevens | W | |

1975/76 season:

8 Aug	**St Helens** (F)	W 17-15	4°
9 Aug	Wigan Sevens	L (in 1st rd)	
15 Aug	**Dewsbury**	W 39-2	4°
22 Aug	**Warrington**	W 25-11	4° (t)
25 Aug	**Swinton**	W 13-2	4°
31 Aug	**Huyton** (LC1)	W 44-17	4° (t)
5 Sep	**Widnes**	W 30-10	4°
14 Sep	Leigh (LC2)	W 23-6	4°
23 Sep	St Helens (LCsf)	W 21-8	4°
26 Sep	**Mayfield** (JP1)	W 57-3	4°
30 Sep	Wigan (FT prelim rd)	D 14-14	4°
4 Oct	Widnes (LCf at Wigan)	L 7-16	4°
7 Oct	**Wigan** (FT replay)	L 19-25	4°
10 Oct	**Australia** (F)	L 6-44	6°
17 Oct	**Castleford**	W 18-10	4° (2t)
2 Nov	Huddersfield	W 40-13	4°
9 Nov	**Oldham** (JP2)	W 46-3	4° (t)
16 Nov	Oldham	W 37-10	4° (2t)
23 Nov	**Workington T** (JP3)	W 16-8	4°
28 Nov	**Featherstone Rovers**	W 13-7	4° (t)
7 Dec	Bradford Northern	W 12-11	4° (t)
13 Dec	**Hull** (JPsf)	L 14-22	4°
22 Dec	**Wakefield Trinity**	L 9-16	4°
26 Dec	Widnes	L 14-19	4°
28 Dec	**Bradford Northern**	W 20-10	4° (t)
1 Jan	**Oldham**	D 8-8	4°
3 Jan	Leeds	L 14-28	4°
11 Jan	Warrington	L 7-8	4°
16 Jan	**Keighley**	W 20-10	4°
25 Jan	Wakefield Trinity	W 13-4	4° (t)
3 Feb	**Wigan**	W 36-20	4° (2t)
6 Feb	Castleford	W 19-16	4°
14 Feb	Castleford (RLC1)	W 25-3	4°
20 Feb	**Leeds**	W 7-5	4°
29 Feb	**St Helens** (RLC2)	L 11-17	4°
2 Apr	**Hull Kingston R**	W 19-3	4° (2t)
9 Apr	**Huddersfield**	W 24-9	4°
25 Apr	Keighley	W 18-10	4°
30 Apr	**Hull KR** (PT1)	W 21-6	4°
11 May	**Wakefield Trinity** (PTsf-1st leg	W 10-5	4°
16 May	Wakefield Trinty (PTsf-2nd leg)	W 14-5	4° (t)
22 May	St Helens (PTf at Swinton)	L 2-15	4°

1976/77 season:

13 Aug	**Swinton** (F)	W 36-8	4°
17 Aug	**Dewsbury** (F)	W 39-11	4°
22 Aug	**Huyton** (LC1)	W 46-14	4°
29 Aug	Warrington (LC2)	L 13-14	4°
3 Sep	**Warrington**	W 16-5	4°
12 Sep	Featherstone Rovers	W 23-12	4°
18 Sep	Widnes	L 12-15	4° (t)
24 Sep	**Hull Kingston R**	D 16-16	4° (t)
28 Sep	Leigh (FT1)	L 18-22	4°

3 Oct	Wigan	L 15-32	4° (t)
8 Oct	**Rochdale Hornets**	W 33-6	4° (t)
17 Oct	Wakefield Trinity	W 18-12	4° (2t)
24 Oct	**Ace Amateurs** (JP1)	W 39-15	4°
29 Oct	**St Helens**	L 15-18	4°
28 Nov	Bradford Northern	L 16-25	14° (nu)
5 Dec	**Wakefield Trinity**	W 22-13	4° (t)
12 Dec	Warrington	L 10-44	4°
19 Dec	**Leigh**	L 12-13	4°
26 Dec	**Widnes**	L 9-13	4°
2 Jan	**Oldham**	W 33-12	4°
9 Jan	Hull Kingston Rovers	L 10-15	4°
14 Jan	**Workington Town**	W 17-5	4° (t)
23 Jan	Leigh	W 45-8	4° (t)
30 Jan	**Barrow**	W 38-13	4° (2t)
5 Feb	Leeds	W 28-13	4° (t)
11 Feb	**Huddersfield** (RLC1)	W 25-2	6°
27 Feb	Workington (RLC2)	L 4-13	4°
6 Mar	St Helens	L 9-29	4°
11 Mar	**Featherstone Rovers**	L 17-18	4°
24 Mar	Workington Town	W 12-6	4°
27 Mar	Rochdale Hornets	L 10-11	6°
3 Apr	Oldham	W 37-8	4°
8 Apr	Barrow	W 15-12	4°
11 Apr	**Wigan**	W 14-10	4°
15 Apr	**Castleford**	W 12-7	4°
22 Apr	**Bradford Northern**	W 32-2	4°
24 Apr	**Leeds**	L 2-5 (aban.)	4°
1 May	Castleford (PT1)	L 17-25	4° (t)
22 May	Swinton Sevens	L (in s-f)	

1977/78 season:

9 Aug	**Leigh** (F)	W 23-15	4°
14 Aug	Swinton (F)	W 35-15	3°
30 Aug	**New Hunslet** (FT preliminary round)	W 39-5	14°
2 Sep	**Featherstone Rovers**	W 7-3	14° (nu)
11 Sep	Bradford Northern	L 14-35	14°
14 Sep	Warrington	W 17-14	3°
18 Sep	New Hunslet	W 17-14	4°
25 Sep	**Warrington**	W 21-10	4° (t)
2 Oct	Dewsbury	W 20-10	4°
4 Oct	Whitehaven (FT1)	W 6-5	4°
7 Oct	**New Hunslet**	W 30-12	4° (t)
21 Oct	**Rochdale H** (JP1)	W 27-8	4°
28 Oct	**Hull Kingston R**	W 23-9	4°
1 Nov	**Oldham** (FT2)	W 29-10	4°
6 Nov	Warrington (JP2)	L 10-19	4° (t)
27 Nov	St Helens	L 12-13	4°
4 Dec	**Castleford**	W 37-8	4°
6 Dec	St Helens (FTsf)	L 4-7	4°
9 Dec	Hull Kingston Rovers	L 10-13	4°
18 Dec	**Wakefield Trinity**	W 21-9	4°
26 Dec	Widnes	L 10-16	4°
1 Jan	**Workington Town**	L 13-19	4°
3 Feb	**Leeds**	W 21-3	4°
24 Feb	**Bramley** (RLC1)	W 9-7	4°

3 Mar	Hull	W 27-18	4°
12 Mar	Huddersfield (RLC2)	L 3-13	4°
21 Mar	St Helens	L 11-24	4°
5 Apr	Bradford Northern	W 21-13	4° (t)
23 Apr	Hull	L 4-18	4°
30 Apr	St Helens (PT1)	L 11-29	4°
21 May	Salford XIII v Welsh XIII (F, at Cwmbran)	W 40-39	4°
1978/79 season:			
6 Aug	Leigh (F)	L 10-16	3 (t)
8 Aug	**Swinton** (F)	W 21-2	4
13 Aug	Blackpool B (F)	W 31-0	4
18 Aug	**Oldham** (LC1)	W 30-15	4
27 Aug	Whitehaven (LC2)	W 19-6	4
1 Sep	**Featherstone Rovers**	W 24-10	6
6 Sep	Huddersfield	W 25-10	6
9 Sep	Leeds	L 16-30	6
13 Sep	**Workington** (LCsf)	L 8-9	6
22 Sep	**Rochdale H** (JP1)	W 25-7	4 (t)
29 Sep	**Bradford Northern**	W 17-8	6
13 Oct	**Hull Kingston R**	L 14-19	4
22 Oct	Leigh	W 31-2	14 (nu)
27 Oct	**Workington Town**	L 8-24	14
1 Nov	**Australia** (tour)	L 2-14	4°
7 Nov	Widnes	L 5-16	6°
12 Nov	Wakefield Trinity	D 10-10	4
17 Nov	**Barrow**	W 24-7	4°
24 Nov	Castleford	L 10-34	4
26 Dec	**Widnes**	D 10-10	6
23 Jan	**Rochdale Hornets**	L 4-13	6
2 Feb	**Leigh**	L 15-22	4
27 Feb	Bramley (RLC1 replay)	D 2-2	6
1 Mar	Bramley (RLC1 2nd replay at Swinton)	L 5-7	6
9 Mar	**Leeds**	L 0-3	6°
23 Mar	**Wakefield Trinity**	L 6-15	4
1 Apr	Rochdale Hornets	W 8-5	6
3 Apr	Bradford Northern	W 12-8	14 (nu)
6 Apr	**Huddersfield**	W 38-3	14
16 Apr	**Wigan**	W 23-15	14
19 Apr	Workington Town	L 0-5	14
22 Apr	Barrow	L 3-23	14
29 Apr	Featherstone Rovers	L 8-20	4 (t)
12 May	Wigan	W 26-13	6
13 May	St Helens	L 4-26	6°
20 May	**Swinton** (F)	W 27-20	4